Best wishes

SPIRIT HEALING

SPIRIT HEALING

By

HARRY EDWARDS

*President: National Federation
of Spiritual Healers*

LONDON: HERBERT JENKINS

First published by
Herbert Jenkins Ltd.
3 Duke of York Street,
London, S.W.1
1960

© HARRY EDWARDS 1960
REPRINTED 1960

MADE AND PRINTED IN GREAT BRITAIN BY
CHARLES BIRCHALL & SONS LTD.
LONDON AND LIVERPOOL

CONTENTS

LIST OF ILLUSTRATIONS

AUTHOR'S NOTE

As this book is about to be printed comes news of a great advance in the recognition of spiritual healing by medicine.

In September 1959 a letter was addressed to each of the London hospital authorities from the National Federation of Spiritual Healers asking permission for its accredited members to go into the hospitals under their management for the purpose of giving healing when requested by patients, subject to the usual medical considerations at the time of the visit. Such treatment would be given by means of prayerful intercession and the laying-on of hands.

By November 30 no less than twenty-two of these authorities granted this permission, which means that approximately two hundred London hospitals have now officially opened their doors to spiritual healers. A Ministry of Health spokesman said that this privilege would be granted on the same basis as that accorded to ministers of religion.

When the first public announcement of this forward movement was made, a representative of the British Medical Association expressed opposition to the scheme, but after this Association was informed in detail of the Federation's intentions and the code of ethics to be adopted by healers attending patients in hospital, the Assistant Secretary of the British Medical Association wrote that the proposals would allay their apprehensions. He went so far as to make a practical suggestion to strengthen the Federation's request to other hospitals.

It is intended to approach every other hospital authority in the United Kingdom and it is confidently expected that the rest of the hospitals will follow London's lead.

Thus for the first time in our history shall we see a form of co-operation exist between the medical fraternity and spiritual healers. This will have far-reaching effects. One will be the need for the revision by the British Medical Council of its veto upon doctors who desire to co-operate with spiritual healers. Another will be that as doctors and surgeons observe the progress made by patients receiving spiritual healing, so will they become more inclined to welcome this healing for the sick ones under their care.

The most important result will be the recognition of the truth of the existence of man's spiritual faculties, proving that he must be part spirit now to be able to receive help from a spirit source, thus providing a new field for medical research.

PART ONE: SPIRIT HEALING

THE HEALING POTENTIAL

Spirit healing is not mysterious, though we may tend to make it so. The most important lesson that I have learned from my healing experiences of over a quarter of a century is that as far as the healer is concerned the healing act is one of simplicity, but its administration is an exact science.

During the past decade the recognition of spiritual healing has made tremendous progress and this has been built upon success in healing the sick. It is now accepted in principle by the Church and the medical profession. The national press recognise it and do not now report healing services or healings for they are no longer "news." More important still, it is enthroned in the homes of people who have witnessed their dear ones restored to health, often when medical science could do no more for them. This recognition is not confined to the United Kingdom; it is spreading throughout the world, particularly in the Dominions and the U.S.A., while Continental prejudices are yielding to the healing forces that are at work.

The sceptic who may think that it is only the credulous and impressionable people who testify to spirit healing will have to account for the fact that people in all walks of life have come to the author for healing. These include members of our Royal Family, and other royal families; cabinet ministers, Privy Councillors, members of the House of Lords, including the leader of one of our national political parties, members of Parliament; an Army Commander in Chief, as well as generals and admirals. Almost every profession is represented, eminent surgeons and physicians, and

11

many doctors. I received over one thousand letters from doctors last year, and many more from ministers of religion, leading to visits to my sanctuary from leaders of Christian thought. There have been Indian princes, an Archbishop, judges and others belonging to the legal profession; conductors of national orchestras, musicians, Olympic athletes, B.B.C. commentators and many names that are household words in the film and theatrical world, and indeed from every phase of life, from the highest ranks down to the most humble. Yet all are equal in healing.

It is not possible to reveal the names of these eminent people, for the great majority are living and all healing is given in confidence. But I can give as illustrations the names of two members of our Royal Family who have passed to spirit life, the Earl of Athlone and H.R.H. Princess Marie Louise. The Princess came a score of times to the Sanctuary, first for the healing of arthritis in her knees and shoulders, which soon yielded, and then for strength and healing for any other trouble that arose. The Princess would ask for absent healing to be given to those in her circle who were in need, including the ex-Queen of Spain, and on her visits she would insist on giving her reports of the progress each one had made.

She came two days before the Coronation of the Queen for strength and help to assist her throughout the tiring receptions and ceremonies. As time went on, age was taking its toll and she became physically very weak. Her last visit occurred shortly before her passing. She was about to have her book published and her request was for just enough strength to go to the Foyle's luncheon to launch the publication. On her arrival she was so weak that she had to be assisted from the car into my lounge. She had not the strength to go the short distance to the Sanctuary. Yet after Mrs. Burton* and I had sought strength for her, she was able to stand erect and to walk back alone to her car. She had her wish and attended the luncheon. Official acknowledgment of the healing help we were able to give to her was made by an invitation from the Lord Chamberlain for me to attend her funeral service in St. George's Chapel, Windsor.

* She and her husband are my collaborators.

The list of eminent people who have sought spiritual healing is not mentioned for any egotistical reason but simply to show how widely accepted the subject has become by persons of intellect in the United Kingdom. It can also be said that others, in all ranks of life, have travelled to the Sanctuary for healing from all the Dominions, the U.S.A. and other countries.

Our understanding of the healing forces is as yet limited, but there are sufficient data and proof, by experience, to enable primary conclusions to be formed to indicate the source and the means of their administration.

These healing forces are not physical. They come from the spirit realm. This fact is a direct challenge to all who are wedded to a purely materialist conception of life; it is, therefore a means by which we can demonstrate in this scientific age the existence of the living spirit and soul of mankind.

There are no set rules or any human technique that controls spirit healing. It comes from another dimension of life, which makes it as difficult for us to comprehend its detailed operation as it is to describe a colour to a man blind from birth. But recent scientific knowledge in connection with the formation and purposes of energy (as with nuclear fission) has contributed towards making our understanding of the healing forces a little clearer.

I define the term "spirit healing" as denoting a healing that is brought about by a non-human agency. While it is a common experience with healers to witness the recovery of sick people from all manner of diseases, we are compelled to prove our case through the healing of those who are deemed to be medically incurable. Proof cannot be satisfactorily established with the healing of more minor conditions, for it may well be said, "The patient would have got well anyway," or "The patient's recovery is attributable to medical or home treatment."

The records of healing testify to a very great number of so-called incurables who have been restored to normal health. Even the British Medical Association now agrees that "through spirit heal-ing recoveries take place that cannot be explained by medical science."* When as a direct result of spirit healing we see mastery established over "incurable" diseases that are beyond the wit of our medical men to accomplish, we establish the *prima facie* evidence for the reality of spirit healing.

In these early pages it is well to define what is believed to be the source of spirit healing, and its administration. We believe that all healing is divine, and that it originates with God. It is part of His plan to show that man is a spiritual being and the way in which the evil of disease can be overcome.

Study of ancient and contemporary religions reveals stories of spirit presences and, as the Bible relates, of the appearance of angels, visions, prophets and voices. During the past century there has been considerable advancement in the development of the awareness and usage of the "gifts of the spirit" and with this the personalities of the spirit guides has become an accepted part of psychic science.

While we have no direct reference to spirit guides in Christ's mission on earth, this does not mean they were not present. We only have to recall the vision of Elisha, the spirit presences at the Pentecostal meeting and the voice that came to Saul.

With the development of modern Spiritualism attention has been focused upon the encouragement for the spirit guides to make themselves known; and this has been done and forms part of the progress of mediumship and healership, thus bringing about a closer affinity between the realm of spirit and ourselves.

The main branches of Christian religion do not acknowledge the good work that has followed the co-operation of these good spirit counsellors to assist, guide and heal sickness in our way of life, but they admit their existence. The Churches disparagingly describe them as "disembodied spirits". At the same time the Anglican Church believes in the "Communion of Saints" and the Roman Catholic Church likewise; and the latter issues medallions representing named saints to protect its members from illness, accidents while travelling, and for other purposes too.

* The B.M.A.s' Report, "Divine Healing and Co-operation between Doctors and Clergy," 1956, and in "The Churches' Ministry of Healing," 1958.

The order of sainthood is conferred by man; it is not a divine ordination and the fact that the Roman Catholic and Anglican Churches believe that these saints can confer blessings and particular benefits on the human family brings their acceptance of the principle that the spirit guides are as real as we know them to be.

The Church admits that disembodied and evil spirits can adversely influence some people; indeed it has prepared services of "exorcism". Therefore it naturally follows that as there are bad spirit influences there are also the good ones, who are part of the heavenly host, dedicated to the furtherance of the Divine plan in a practical way by awakening man's spiritual consciousness through the demonstrable acts of curing minds, bodies and souls of their imperfections and the taking away of disease and pain.

In recent years nearly every main branch of Christian religion in the United Kingdom, the Church of England, Church of Scotland, Presbyterians, Congregationalists and the Methodists, have conducted commissions of enquiry into spirit healing. They have examined the claims for healing with great care. In every case the investigation lasted a number of years—in the case of the Church of England it was five years. The terms of reference for each commission was to verify that spirit healings are factual and to try and discover how the lost gift of healing could be revived in the pastoral work of the churches. With the second directive we are not concerned, but with the first it is noteworthy to record that in every one of the reports it was recognised that spirit healings have taken place contrary to medical expectations, through the healership of lay men and women who are not members of the respective denominations.

Our purpose is to examine and ascertain on what basis it rests, how others may develop the gift of healing, and to understand its limitations as well as its capabilities.

With all persons of good will the desire to heal the sick is a hope and a prayer, but its attainment seems out of reach, just a dream. Yet we will endeavour to show that with those who possess the inner yearning to heal it is by no means so unattainable as may at first be thought.

I became aware of my healing potential in an unexpected
fashion. Prior to 1935 I was a Liberal advocate and a parliamen-
tary candidate, with a burning desire to work for peace and social
security. I had never given a thought to spirit healing. I had, of
course, known of Spiritualism. Apart from attending one church
service in 1922, which impressed me greatly, I viewed Spiritualism
with a very critical eye. In fact, I believed it to be little more than
an unfounded belief in the supernatural which did not exist. My
outlook at the time was that of a Rationalist, with little regard for
religion.

In 1935 a friend asked if I would go to a small Spiritualist
church held in a private house near to where I lived. I did so with
an open mind but very determined not to be hoodwinked and to
consider everything in the light of common sense. I received a
number of messages from mediums stating that I possessed the
healing gift. So I attended two church developing circles, where
I again received encouragement to utilise my gift of healing. It was
at one of these circles that I conducted my first experiment in healing. My friend told me that a male acquaintance of hers was lying
in Brompton Hospital dying from galloping consumption and
pleurisy. Severe hæmorrhages were taking place. He was not
expected to live very long. Together we concentrated upon this
man that he should receive healing and be made well. As I did
this a picture was presented to my mind of a hospital ward with its
rows of beds. In the second bed from the end was our patient.
Later I received full confirmation that the vision given to me was a
true picture of the patient and the ward he was in.

When we next met, a week later, I enquired how our patient
was, and was gratified to learn that the pleurisy had gone, his
temperature had come down to normal and the bleedings had
ceased. We continued our concentrations. The outcome was that
within three weeks the man was so much better that he was sent to
a convalescent home. In a comparatively short time he was back
in his employment.

Not long afterwards a woman came into my shop where I was
conducting a printing and stationery business. She was very dis-

tracted and said she had been impelled to enter the shop without knowing the reason why. She unburdened her grief to me. Her husband had been an in-patient in a London hospital, where it was discovered he was suffering from an advanced cancer of the lung. He was in a chronic state of weakness. The doctors said they could do no more for him, so they had sent him home by ambulance. The wife was informed that he was dying and told to make him as comfortable as possible.

To assuage her grief I told her that I would seek spirit healing for him. I did so that night, feeling, however, that it was far too much to hope for a cure to take place. Two days later she called on me with a wonderful story. The first morning after I had told her I would seek healing for her husband he had got up early and made her a cup of tea. A great change was apparent in him. The children were sent for, just to see the change. They sat and looked at him in amazement. When the man again attended the hospital he was seen by a new doctor, who, after examining him, congratulated him upon the success of the medical treatment. When the doctor was informed that the man had received no treatment at all, he refused to believe that the diagnosis in the medical history applied to the patient. Soon he was back at work, and to my knowledge was alive some twenty years later. It is interesting to note that this man was an agnostic, and his wife dared not tell him either about the seriousness of his illness or the means by which he was assisted to recover. Thus my first two cases were of "absent healing" given without the patient's knowledge.

The third case was one of contact healing. The sister of a very sick girl received a message from a clairvoyant to seek me out. This she did, knocking at my door very late at night. She told me her story, how her sister was very ill with a high temperature and the doctor was apprehensive about her. As she lived in a nearby street I promised to go and see her the next day and to ask for healing to reach her that night.

When I called at the house next morning, I found that straw had been strewn in the road outside to lessen all traffic noises. The curtains were almost drawn and the room was in semi-darkness.

I laid my hands upon the girl's forehead and sought for strength and healing to be given to her. This was a Thursday morning. As I treated her I knew intuitively that she would get better. I remember telling the mother, in my innocence, that I thought her daughter would be up by the weekend. I still recall the incredulous look on the mother's face. My prediction was fulfilled. The fever left the girl, who was able to sit up and drink tea on the Sunday.

The story does not end there, for I was then informed that she had tuberculosis. One lung had a cavity and had been collapsed and she was receiving fortnightly refills of air. I continued the healing for this trouble. The cavity disappeared and she could not take any further refills. When she returned for examination to the sanatorium where she had previously been given medical treatment, it was found that the cavity had completely healed. All her tests were negative. She was given a clean bill of health. Later she became a nurse in the same sanatorium where she had been a patient less than a year before. This girl never suffered again. She married, has a grown-up family and is fully well today.

These three cases proved to me that there was "something" in healing. Coincidence was ruled out. I continued to seek the development of my healing gift. Other successful treatments followed. Before long, I opened my house as a healing sanctuary where the sick came in ever-increasing numbers.

My further experiences in development will be told in a later chapter. These early happenings are narrated for the purpose of showing readers that in the beginning I did not intentionally seek the healing gift and that it was more or less forced upon me by design and circumstance. Others, with a similar latent gift, may be encouraged to read further.

I feel it necessary first to set out the fundamental postulates upon which healing rests and to show the processes by which those who are sick can be helped by an understanding of man's physical and spirit make-up.

Suffice it for now to state that it is abundantly clear that the human instrument does not possess any healing faculties of himself (except in the aid that can be given through his affinity with the patient) and that there are no human techniques that can heal. One cannot develop the healing gift by study, as is done in other physical arts and sciences. The gift of healing cannot be conferred by a degree, by ordination, or by the wearing of a white coat. It functions when those who have the faculty establish attunement with God's healing ministers in Spirit who indeed are the intelligent administrators of this beneficent power.

CHAPTER TWO

THE TOTAL SELF

Before there is any understanding of the ways and means of spirit healing, and the postulates which govern its operation, it is essential to have a picture of the physical and spirit combinations that go to the make-up of the total self, and the means by which co-operation and attunement with Spirit can be attained.

Man possesses a counterpart of the physical body which we call the "spirit body". It is the perfect body, and acts as the vehicle for the spirit self in spirit life, just as our physical body is the vehicle for our material life.

In addition to the physical mind, each individual also possesses a spirit mind. This has been referred to in many terms, the psyche, the "I", the soul, and so on. The physical mind has as its concern the sensing and appreciation of physical sensation, comfort, sexual expression, direction of the organic systems and the gathering and garnering of earthly knowledge.

The spirit mind is concerned with the higher and baser motives of life, idealism and ambitions, emotions, love, hatred, generosity, meanness, etc.

The consciousness is the meeting place for both minds. It is where the self become conscious of impressions, directives and experiences. The physical mind can influence the spirit mind for good or ill, otherwise there could be no progression; conversely the spirit mind can motivate the other.

Just as the physical mind is in intimate attunement with our bodily needs and sensations and is the reservoir of gathered knowledge, so the spirit mind can be in attunement with thought and guidance from spirit life. This is an important conclusion upon which much of our understanding of spirit science depends.

The proof that we possess a spirit mind is easily established by the simple comparative study of the processes of physical and spirit sensing.

Everything we experience is a mental appreciation, pain, hunger, comfort, sight, hearing, etc. For example, the eye itself does not "see." It receives characterised light reflections on the thousands of rods and cones comprising the retina. From each rod and cone there is a nerve that carries the particular radiation through the optic nerve system, where it is interpreted by the consciousness into a recorded experience, and the many facets of the picture build up the whole vision. A similar process applies to hearing, where the consciousness interprets the many variations of sound waves into recognisable forms of speech, music, etc.

When a clairvoyant sees a spirit personality or picture it is the consciousness which receives this just as precisely as with physical sight. Yet the spirit picture and sounds are not discernible by the bodily eyes and ears.

It is a law that there must exist a state of harmony between any form of transmission and reception. There must be a medium in some form between the origin of the transmission and the organisation for its reception, to permit the flow of radiation to be conducted and accepted. With physical sight and hearing this is readily perceived. With spirit sight and hearing this same basic principle must apply. It follows that a picture transmitted from a spirit source can be received only through an attuned potential in the person, and this must be his spirit mind.

In considering the mechanism of healing, it is important to see that in the same way as spirit sensing is received by the consciousness so "thought" can be received too. Thought impressions can be conveyed from the spirit mind to the consciousness, thus influencing physical mind. In this way the healing guide is able to soothe and calm inner-mind frustrations which are admitted to be the cause of so much disease.

The same reasoning can be applied to all forms of mental reception, such as inspirational thought, intuitions, solutions to problems, etc. When persons are able to cultivate this art we call them mediums and healers. They are not constructed any differently from non-mediumistic people. It is simply that the consciousness of a medium is so attuned as to be able to receive experiences from his spirit mind. As a medium or healer proves the existence of his spirit self, so does every other person possess a spirit mind and body, though psychic awareness may be dormant.

When a person suffering from a disease resulting from spirit mind disharmony receives healing, the good corrective thought influences are directed to overcome it, even though he is not conscious of the act. Yet as the remedial change is induced, the patient's general outlook is lightened and the cause of the disease is removed.

Consideration must also be given to the association of the *body intelligence* with spirit healing. By "body intelligence" I refer to the ordered processes that are called into being when there is a need. For example, when a virus enters the blood-stream the body intelligence calls for the mobilisation of the antidotal qualities in the blood to fight and overcome the invader. When there is a wound, the intelligence will call up sufficient supplies of platelets to bridge the wound, strengthening the processes to heal it. When we hear of people who by the exercise of will power assist the mastering of an ill-condition, we have the application of directive thought to stimulate the body intelligence to adopt active measures to overcome the trouble. Thus it is reasonable to assume that when a spirit guide diagnoses the trouble he is able to direct corrective thought impulses to the body intelligence to act.

Nowhere in creation is there any rigid division between any form of matter and, particularly, living forms of life. There is no division between gases and liquids, liquids and solids, between fish and mammals, and so on. Neither is there any rigid division between the physical and the spirit realm. It is but an extension of this to conclude there is a liaison between the spirit directive, the mind and the bodily intelligence, and therefore the faculty exists where the merging of one with the other takes place.

Thus the body intelligence is receptive to direction not only in a physical way that in the past has been called "nature" or "instinct" but also to directive action inspired from Spirit. This is only one aspect of the healing processes and is additional to the administration of healing forces by direct action to overcome organic disease.

This "direct action" is seen when a growth is dispersed, or arthritic adhesions are dissolved. The operation of these forces follows the study of the postulates which govern healing as outlined in the next chapter.

CHAPTER THREE

POSTULATES THAT GOVERN HEALING

As yet, we possess but little comprehension of how healings take place. We know there are no set rules that govern them. No one healing can be given as a precedent for another. For example, I have seen one deformed foot of a child instantly yield, but the other foot in a seemingly similar state did not. I have witnessed those who have been very dear to me fail to respond, while in the same week a stranger suffering from a more chronic state of the same disease make an outstanding recovery.

There are, however, certain basic conclusions that we can deduce by logic which govern the healing.

The study of healing experiences of the past, with peoples of different nationalities and religions, with those who are advanced in the conduct of human society and the reverse, all disclose one common factor in healing. This factor is that before any healing has taken place there has been a form of thought application for it to do so. It may be by prayer, intercession or by incantation. This is the common denominator that links the Roman Catholics at Lourdes, the Christian Scientist, the Spiritualist and every other form of religion in healing. It appears that a purposeful thought emission is necessary to put the healing processes into action. Spirit healing does not commence by itself automatically or as a matter of right.

I recall a case that is a clear example. The wife of a healer was very ill from a spinal collapse and was due to be encased in plaster on the morrow. On the previous evening I had a sitting with the husband and his children when he went into trance. Naturally the children asked the guide who spoke about their mother. The eldest son was indignant that the guides had not healed her. The significant spirit reply was, "We have never been asked." Whereupon the son said, "Well, I ask you now to help my mother." The guide answered, "We will try." During the night the mother felt her spine being manipulated and she knew she was freed from her trouble. When the specialist arrived in the morning to encase the patient in plaster he found her up and walking about completely well.

Thus the first conclusion is: *there must be the emission of a purposeful thought force to initiate the healing.*

Everything that takes place, every movement, every change within our comprehension is the result of law-governed forces applied to the subject. There is no exception. We witness this in the evolution of matter, the courses of the stars, germination, birth, growth, death, the atomic formation of an element and all else. Human science is based upon these certain laws, otherwise there would be chaos. Nothing takes place by chance or accident. There is no such thing as a miracle.

The same ruling must apply to spirit healings. When a spirit healing takes place, law-governed forces are put into operation therefore, according to the universal principle, healings must be the result of law-governed forces applied to the given condition.

This conclusion introduces one of the limiting factors in healing. No healing can take place if it is contrary to the law. For example, if a finger is amputated a new one cannot be grown, or if advanced age has brought senility the healing cannot restore juvenility. While we maintain the causes of disease then the ill-effects will be sustained. Consider the common case of weakening eyesight due to undue strain imposed by close and exacting work. When this is persisted in a recovery is unlikely. If a sufferer receiving healing for arthritis lives in damp conditions and sleeps in a damp bed, then the arthritis will be encouraged. This need not imply that the healing effort will be entirely negative, for it will maintain the affected condition in as good a state as can be induced, considering the character of the cause. For example, if a person is suffering from hardened arteries due to advancing years, we should not expect to see a restoration to normal conditions, but we do witness a diminution of the trouble and the circulation sustained to the fullest extent possible.

Just as the earthly realm is controlled by the physical laws, so it is logical that the spirit realm is likewise law-governed too, for such must exist wherever there is order. Under the spirit laws there must also be forces that come within their jurisdiction, thus permitting the laws to function.

In spirit healing there is every reason to believe that the guides are able to direct spirit law-governed forces or energies to effect a change for the better in the total self of a patient.

Combining these first two conclusions we see that *spirit healings result from law-governed forces put into operation following the emission of a thought directive.*

The records of healing successes denote a further common factor: whenever the right conditions are created for healings to take effect, the range is limited only by the physical and spirit laws. We see healings take place of very diverse kinds through the instrumentality of one healer. As an example, (a) the restoring of an unbalanced mind, (b) the removal of a malignant growth, (c) the restoration of sight or another sense, (d) the change in the blood content in leukemia, etc. This implies that there is no one healing force, but that a different character of force is necessary for the treatment of each individual complaint.

To apply the right quality of healing force to the respective human disharmony indicates the ability of diagnosis and discrimination. To achieve this there must be a directing and administrative intelligence.

When a sick person is deemed to be incurable it means that human wisdom has become exhausted; medical science can do no more. When through healing the "incurable" recovers and is restored to health, it must mean that a superior intelligence has intervened. As this intelligence is not human it *must* come from Spirit.

Some say that this knowledge comes from the human subconscious mind. There is no evidence that mankind possesses to-day, or ever has possessed, the detailed knowledge to carry out the planned act of healing when human skill can do no more. Therefore there has been no human experience from which the subconscious mind can draw such precise and profound knowledge.

The implication follows that the spirit guides have been able to acquire this wider knowledge. It also implies that to carry out a healing of the physical mind and body this wisdom must not only include the ordered employment of the spirit forces but to know how to combine them with the physical forces that govern the human anatomy, and to be able at some stage to transform a spirit force into a physical effect.

There must be intelligent direction to achieve any planned act, even though it is only building a rabbit hutch. To use any physical force, such as electricity, we must understand the laws that govern it and its potentials. We can then administer them to obtain a given effect. A healing is a planned act; it has both intention and direction. Thus to attain the desired result there must exist the knowledge of how to administer the corrective forces to produce the desired chemical or functional change in the patient.

The acquiring of wisdom by the human faculty has always been through the slow and laborious process of trial and error. It is a logical assumption that the mind of a spirit guide does not suddenly become the possessor of infinite wisdom but that it, too, has had to travel the same road, acquiring, step by step, its greater comprehension of the spirit law-governed forces and how they can be applied to co-operate with the physical forces to produce a beneficial change in the state of a sick person. As evidence for this we have seen the greater ease with which certain diseases yield to spirit healing today than they did in past years.

Here then is the third summary to these conclusions. *That consequent on the emission of a thought appeal by a human mind in attunement with spirit intelligence the spirit guide is able to receive the request and to administer the correct quality of force to heal the particular disharmony in the body of the patient.*

The healing ability of the guides is not omnipotent. As has been said, it is limited by the total law. Thus while instantaneous cures of major ailments are not infrequent, the greater percentage of healings need a period of time to permit the sustained efforts on the part of the guide to overcome progressively the cause of the disease and remove its ill-effects. Many bodily ill-conditions need this time to allow the good changes to take place, to overcome wastages and weaknesses, to build up new strength and vitality, co-ordination, etc. Spirit healing is indeed a spirit science.

In the past, medical authorities have called recoveries from "incurable" diseases that they cannot explain by medical science "spontaneous healings," viewing them as a result of "nature asserting itself"; and they have been content to leave it at that. There must be a reasoned process behind every state of change. It is suggested that the line of reasoning denoted here provides a logical and reasoned thesis to account for recoveries that are contrary to medical expectation.

This book is being written from the Spiritualist standpoint, based on the natural law of survival after death. The critic has either to accept the stated conclusions or provide another thesis based on logic.

CHAPTER FOUR

METHODS OF HEALING

Many people wish to know how they may develop the gift of healing the sick. Healing is perhaps the greatest gift that can be desired; it is certainly the most spiritual one. The healings recorded in the New Testament have stirred the imagination of all ages for the past two thousand years. If one asks the average person which aspect of the life of Jesus is best remembered, the reply will most likely tell of the "miracles," of which the healings are the most impressive.

So it is today that when one comes into close contact with illness and suffering, especially with a relative or a dear friend, one's inner being yearns to be able to restore the sick one to health again.

This desire to heal is a natural talent. Generally speaking, all who inwardly "feel" for those who suffer may possess the healing potential. It is true that there are those who may be termed "natural healers", in the same way that others have a natural aptitude for music, painting, mathematics, etc.

Those who are self-centred, selfish and concerned only with gain for what they do are very unlikely to possess the healing faculty. The motive force behind spiritual healers is that of love and compassion; they are generous in giving without material reward. They love to render service for all their fellows who are in need.

Spirit healing is not new—it is age-old. Jesus knew the way to invoke the healing power, and taught His disciples and others the way to use it. The awareness of this gift has been resurrected in this age, and possibly furthered by our new knowledge of psychic science and the spirit potentials.

29

The first and perhaps the most important lesson the would-be healer must learn is that *he* does not heal. The healer's body possesses no particular qualities that can remove the cause of disease in another. His mind does not possess the knowledge how to do it. There are no techniques to learn. The healer is but the instrument of the spirit guides who use him as a channel for healing through his ability of attunement with them.

There are no set rules that govern healing. Neither is there any one way for the development of the healing gift. Each person is individual to himself and the spirit guides are distinct personalities, too. There are, however, certain general directives that can assist the would-be healer to develop the gift.

The reader will already have observed that the author, supremely conscious of the divine source of spirit healing, is endeavouring to treat this subject from a practical point of view, for the more we understand what we are doing and why we are doing it the greater will be the progress made. Ritual and ceremony and fanciful techniques may impress the credulous, and even such people may benefit in a psychological sense and through the sincere healing intention, but these practices serve no real purpose. Nor are they of the slightest value in the effort to understand the science of healing—they only hamper the good effort.

For the reason that healing comes from another dimension and we cannot, as yet, understand its detailed application or operation, no healer is ever able to foretell in advance what the healing result may be. Therefore it is not within the power of the healer to give any promise or undertaking in advance.

At the same time, the healer should never limit within his mind the power of the spirit to heal. On many occasions I have been presented with a chronic ill-condition. My reasoning mind may think "surely nothing can be done in this case". Yet to my surprise and astonishment I have seen healings take place with these seemingly impossible conditions.

I recall the case of the wife of a Methodist minister who sought healing for weakening sight in her right eye; her left eye had been blind for thirty years. We thought it most unlikely that the blind eye could be helped. No healing was sought for it and attention was paid to the right eye only. Yet when the treatment was finished she could see perfectly well with the left eye. Within a short time of this taking place there was a similar healing of the ear of an Anglican minister which had been stone deaf for many years. Still more remarkable was the case of a young man whose spine was deformed from birth; it showed an acute "S" bend, was hunch-back and completely rigid. My thoughts were that the trouble was so advanced and deep-seated that we could not reasonably expect to see a change take place, but we made the effort. To my surprise I felt the spine begin to yield, become mobile and straighten up.

There have been hundreds of successful healings where one would have been justified in assuming that no benefit could be anticipated, which indicates how little is our knowledge of that which is possible to Spirit within the framework of natural law. Frequently there comes an urgent request by telephone from a very distressed person to ask for help to reach a dear one of whom the doctors have said the end of life is quickly coming and for whom there is no hope. Intercession takes place for the sick one. The next day we are told how the patient has slept restfully and there is a turn for the better which the doctor cannot explain. While we do not see a recovery take place with everyone, the per-centage of success with such chronic cases is by no means negligible.

Suffice it, therefore, to say that the healer must have supreme confidence, all the time, in the spirit guides to heal to the fullest extent that is possible within the law.

There are three main types of healing (i) Magnetic Healing, (ii) Contact Healing, (iii) Absent Healing.

Magnetic Healing

The term "magnetic" healing is often used, but it is an unfor-tunate use of the word. The magnetic force is a polarised physical force and is not a healing force. A better description is "Cosmic Healing."

This form of healing is often given unconsciously, as when a person of robust health and abounding vitality visits a sick one, and the patient feels so much better for his presence. On the other hand some people are able to draw energy from others. One hears the remark, "She seems to sap all the energy out of me."

This form of healing is not spirit healing but the transference of cosmic energy from one to the other. Cosmic energies exist for our well-being and their presence can be simply explained by the analogy of a tree. The tree does not live alone by the nutriment it absorbs through its roots (such nutriment is akin to the food we consume). Its vitality and full health depend upon the cosmic forces that it absorbs through its leaves. Chlorophyll is created in this way. It absorbs the solar rays and those other health-giving forces that eddy about it. Humans do this, too. If they train themselves consciously to absorb these vitalising forces through their breathing they can take in an abundance, thus maintaining their reservoir of inner strength to the full. A further illustration is when we go to the seaside and sense the ozone. We naturally take in deep breaths, for we inwardly know it is strengthening and good for us.

When a "magnetic" healer is in sympathy with a sick one he can consciously direct a flow of his energy to the patient. That is why the patient feels better and stronger. If the healer does this continuously with a number of patients then he, too, will feel depleted until he re-charges his reserves.

All a magnetic healer has to do is to take the patient's hands and through his mental request "give of himself" for the strengthening forces to flow.

The range of disease that can be helped in this way is limited, but indirectly it can help almost all ill-conditions. The complaints that can be helped are chiefly anæmia, nerve and functional disorders, chest weaknesses, and weaknesses consequent on paralysis, the circulation, etc. This healing does not directly overcome disease but gives the body that inner strength and vitality to assist the body intelligence to take advantage of it, to build up the health-tone and permit the healing forces more easily to counteract the disease.

There is no division between magnetic healing and spirit healing
—one can lead to the other. It is often the first step in the development of the healing gift.

Contact Healing

The essential quality for contact healing is attunement between
the healer and the patient and between the healer and the spirit
guide. The healer becomes the channel through which the healing
forces are directed to the patient. It should be recalled that the
patient as well as the healer possesses a spirit mind and body.
Through the healer's love of his mission and his sympathy for the
patient come a blending of both their spirit selves. Thus we have
not only the conscious linking up of healer with patient but also
blending of their spirit selves. It is in this condition of affinity that
the guide directs the remedial healing forces via the healer to the
patient.

The healing force that comes from Spirit must at first be non-
physical, for it comes from a non-material source. But at some
stage it has to be transferred into its physical counterpart, and
it is reasonable to think that this transformation takes place through
the intimate affinity existing between the healer's (or patient's)
spirit body and his physical self.

Absent Healing

Amazing as are the results with other forms of spirit healing,
those obtained by absent healing are at first sight many times more
mystifying. With contact healing there is the tangible human link
with the patient, but with absent healing there is only the intangible medium of thought.

Briefly, absent healing is directed by the healer on behalf of
someone at a distance, generally a person whom the healer has
never seen. The patient may be on the other side of the world;
distance is immaterial.

With absent healing a new factor comes into the picture that totally destroys the argument that spirit healing is the outcome of will-power or "faith" healing. This factor is the introduction of a third party or intermediary, such as when a relative or a friend applies for help for someone else. The necessity for the third party is created by the patient being too weak to write, a child, even a baby, a person who is being kept ignorant of his disease or when the patient and his family are opposed on religious or other grounds to receive healing from a Spiritualist. In these circumstances there is no direct contact between the healer and the patient, so there can be no question of self-will or faith.

The application for healing is either made orally or in writing. When the healer receives the request, he seeks attunement with the spirit guide and conveys the request with all the information that he has. The intercession usually takes place when the healer can sit by himself (or with friends) in seclusion and silence. He divorces from his mind all considerations of a material nature and attunes to the spirit guide. The healer has the supreme confidence that in this state of attunement the spirit guides receive the appeal and data on behalf of the patient. As the healer progresses in his development so does the ease of attunement become as second nature.

There is no limit to the nature of diseases which can be cured or relieved by spirit healing (within the total laws) and this also applies to absent healing.

Having received the information the healing guide has then to contact the patient. This act may be more difficult for us to comprehend than actually is the case.

As the spirit-self of the medium is able to travel in an instant to the patient (see the reference to "spirit travelling" later in this chapter), so is the spirit intelligence easily able to seek out the sick one. The weight of evidence to support absent healing is now so vast that we are compelled to accept the fact that such contact is made, otherwise the healings could not take place. In the author's case, absent healing forms by far the greater portion of his healing and thousands of cases are dealt with each week.

The healing guide will then make his diagnosis of the trouble and its cause, his attention being first directed to overcoming the cause and then to removing the symptoms of stress.

Causes of trouble are mainly two-fold. Those of purely physical origin, such as a broken limb, and those that are the product of mind and inner-self disharmony. It is now admitted by all authorities that the major percentage of diseases have their primary causation in some form of mental stress or spirit-self frustration. As the physical and spirit minds are so akin to each other, the guide's task of diagnosis is more easy than may at first be appreciated. Further, for the reason that the patient's spirit minds are open to corrective influencing by the spirit guides, it is logical to assume they can diagnose the causes of trouble far more easily than our doctors.

With absent healing and, indeed, with all other forms of healing, there is one condition of mind on the part of the healer which must be avoided, that is *casualness*. Healing cannot be expected as a matter of right. Therefore a purposeful directive should always be maintained in intercession.

Some healers make it a rule to intercede for a patient at a set time each day. The patient is requested to try and link up in thought at this particular time for healing to reach him. The author discontinued this practice after a V.1 bomb destroyed his home and all his carefully kept time appointments. I expected the healing to suffer as a result, but I found that instead of slackening there came reports of even greater progress with the sick ones. On considering why this should be, I recalled that to establish attunement with Spirit the mind must be calm and free from stress. My watching the clock did not help and I realised that the spirit healing did not need to be disciplined by following a time-table. Furthermore, it meant that the patients would have to arrange for their domestic affairs to be completed before the time appointment. The patient who may be troubled by pain would only induce a state of acute mental stress in his expectancy of easement. With his mind being strongly possessed by stressful thoughts he was actually in the worst possible condition to receive healing.

This is the procedure we adopt at the Sanctuary for absent

healing. When the post arrives the letters are put through a letter opener and the contents taken out. They are then read by my co-operating healers and myself. The character of reply is indicated by code references and personal annotations made on the letters. All new applications and cases of serious illness are passed to me. With my co-operators, long experience has brought the art of attunement between us and the guides into an ever-present condition, so that even when the letters are read and answered the intercession takes place as we convey to the listening-in guide the progress and further need of the patient. The time needed for this is just that which is sufficient for our minds to convey the "picture". For those who are responding well and getting better this is all that is needed. The letters are then passed on to experienced typists to convey the answers we have indicated.

With those patients whose troubles are deep-seated and serious, they are put aside for the intercessions that take place in the late evening and early morning hours.

As the "proof of the pudding is in the eating" so the proof of our methods is in the results. At each time we have taken an analysis of the healings we have found the figures consistent, that is, that over eighty per cent. of the reports indicate improvements with stressful conditions yielding. Of these, in time, over thirty per cent. report complete recoveries. These figures are significant when it is recalled that people do not generally write to us for minor troubles that can be dealt with at home or by the doctor.

The twenty per cent. who do not report improvement does not mean that no help has been received. For example, when a passing takes place with a painful disease, such as malignant cancer, we are invariably told that with the healing the patient became restful, had peaceful sleep and the passing was devoid of any form of stress. While we register such a case within the twenty per cent. of non-healing, there is no question that help was given more than mere words can tell.

So, to-day, our intercessions take place from late at night and in the small hours of the morning when it is hoped the patients are asleep with their minds at rest. This has the further advantage that as the healer is in a continuous state of attunement he is able to receive intuitively directions how to counsel the patient to take advantage of the healing progress.

Once a healing has started it does not stop. Therefore it is wise for the patient to keep the healer informed of the progress being made by regular reports, so that he may have as complete a mind-picture of the patient's condition as can be. During the healer's intercession he conveys this mind-picture to the guide and purposeful continuity is maintained.

When the healer, in silence and seclusion, is able to tune in more deeply he may sometimes become aware of the experience known as "astral" or "spirit" travelling. What happens is this. As the healer's spirit mind becomes ascendant, and he is concerned with the healing needs of say, Mr. Brown of Oxford, who is suffering from tuberculosis, there becomes pictured on his consciousness a vision of the room, with all its details where the patient is staying. These visions are more precise, vivid and lasting than with natural vision and memory. It is as if the healer were actually in the room. The picture may last only for a few seconds, but it is so firmly embedded on the healer's consciousness that it can be recalled just as vividly any time afterwards. The author can now recall experiences of this nature that occurred twenty years ago. Whenever steps have been taken to verify the accuracy of such vision in detail, full corroboration has been given.

There are also many recorded experiences where the patient has "seen" the presence of the healer in his room, and it is only later when a patient sees a photograph of the healer, or meets him, that the healer's features are recognised.

A small boy was ill, and his father asked for absent healing for him. A full recovery followed. It so happened that the father took his son to a healing service where I was demonstrating. The boy became excited, and shouted, "Look, that is the man I saw in my bedroom when I was ill!"

When spirit travelling takes place the healer is conscious of his presence with the patient in an instant. There is no sensation of travelling a distance. He is just there. The explanation is simple.

It is the healer's spirit mind that travels to the patient with whom he is in tune with at the time. Therefore as this can take place with the healer's spirit self, it becomes clearer that the guide, quite at home in his realm of activity, is also able to contact a patient when the call for help is made by absent healing.

Spiritual healers are often asked, "How do you feel when a healing is taking place?" or, "What are your feelings when you know that a healing has taken place?"

To understand the basis of a healer's feeling one must appreciate the motive of his mission. Healing is a personal gift, which can belong only to those whose natures are compassionate and who radiate love in themselves, express it for others and in their way of life. They are generous in giving, possessing the aptitude to render service in the name of God and humanity even if this entails a personal sacrifice. With some people the gift is dormant but it can be awakened through the development of attunement with the spirit realm.

You will never find a healer who is mean, selfish and arrogant, one who will never give of himself unless he can get something out of it. The gift of healing is therefore a spiritual quality that arises from a spiritual nature. This does not mean that a healer needs to be "churchy", for spirituality is the expression of natural love, goodness and generosity. I have said before that if I were to look for angels on earth, I should not go to the bishops' palaces, or to Mayfair, but into the homes of ordinary people where, so often, adversity in life promotes that "giving of the self" in service to a friend in need. I think of the mother who denies herself for her children and, hard worked as she may be, is ever ready to take food to a sick neighbour, or help to keep her house clean, even if it is only washing the doorstep.

Because the healer has love and compassion for the sick, a deep inner yearning to take away the pains and anguish, the realisation that a healing has taken place fulfils his desire and lifts him into a happiness that cannot be adequately described in words . . . at least, I cannot.

The writer has known both sorrow and hardship, and has experienced many of the normal joys of life. But there are no joys that can transcend the healer's feeling when a joint locked by arthritis becomes free, or that intuitive knowledge that a very sick one, near to passing, will obtain new strength and get well.

The gift of healing creates a feeling that is quite different to all other human experiences. The healer knows he has "something", an inner strength and spirit companionship that makes him realise he is not just a human being but a man with plus "something," a linking-up with an intangible but positive fellowship with the good people on the other side of the veil.

Let me illustrate from my own experiences. There have been very rare occasions when I have sat down to heal a person and felt "nothing" with me. Something very vital was missing. The patient and me. I could not blend. He was just a stranger with whom I had no affinity. When I attempted to ease his pain or stiffness it appeared to be no more than trying to help or move an inanimate thing. On the rare occasions this has happened I stop trying to heal for a time. I sit quietly and await the coming of attunement, that comforting and reassuring feeling of being encompassed or possessing in my whole self the conviction that I am not alone.

Human nature has its peculiarities. Most people can recall occasions when meeting someone for the first time they feel repelled by his personality that they shrink from him. I recall an occasion that has nothing to do with healing. It occurred when I kept a stationer's shop. A man came in for something. As I looked at him I could not help but feel a very bitter antagonism towards him. His very being repelled me. I had never seen him before. I knew, too, that he sensed my revulsion of feeling and that he felt similarly towards me. I felt within myself that he was evil. Some time later he returned to my shop, not to buy anything, but to ask why he and I felt like that towards each other. The strange thing is that as we talked so this bitterness left me, and him too. It would take too long to discuss the "why" and the "wherefore" of this change and how it came about. It provides an interesting problem for the psychologist. To answer it simply, a spiritual change must have come to one or both of us to overcome the feelings of animosity.

On only two occasions do I remember this aversion to another during the quarter of a century I have been healing. The first occurred over twenty years ago, but I can recall it very vividly. A woman came to my house to learn if I could heal her deafness. She explained that when she was a baby her mother had poured hot oil into her ears and from that time she had been stone deaf. As I sat before her, I could not help feeling a repugnance towards her. I did not feel that I could help her, but I made the effort and placed my hands over her ears and sought healing for her—but apparently with no result. At ten o'clock that same night came a loud knocking on my door. On opening it, there was the woman in an excited state. All she could say was, "I can hear!" "I can hear!". There is a humorous sequel to this story. Some three days later, she again came to see me. She told me that she worked in a laundry and she never thought that the girls she worked with could swear so much.

The other case of aversion also had a happy healing result. This shows that spiritual healing is superior to the lesser feelings we may be conscious of from time to time.

I believe that harmony and blending between healer and patient are of primary importance. It is in this way that affinity between the healer's and the patient's spirit-selves is attained, which helps so much in establishing mutual understanding, confidence and sympathy and consequently the healing itself.

If healers did not have this inner feeling of goodness and yearning to heal. If they did not look forward to the healing occasions as the greatest event of the day or week, they would not take the trouble to use their time in this way. Can it be thought reasonable that any person who does not possess these yearnings to heal would give up their free time, after an arduous day's work, to enter an atmosphere of illness, to meet the sick with whom there is nothing in common and who may be depressed or in pain, unless there does exist this "healing feeling" that defies explanation but which is truly a spiritual quality?

"Healing feelings" therefore are apart from all the other normal human emotions of recreational enjoyment, hobbies, theatre-going, picnics, or basking in the seaside sands in the sunshine. It is different from the affection for dear ones. These are good, pleasurable and satisfying to our physical selves. But any healer will tell you they are lesser compared with the exquisite joy in seeing pain relieved, the sick made well and, even more than this, the joyous anticipation and realisation of being the means to cure disease.

CHAPTER FIVE

THE HEALING GIFT

It has already been said, and it is worth repeating, that the healer does not heal of himself or by reason of any technique or ritual that he may adopt. The healing directive comes from Spirit. The development of the healing gift therefore is dependent upon the state of affinity or attunement that can be established between the healer and his spirit guides.

Many healers obtain their preliminary development in a home or church circle under the guidance of an experienced medium. The purpose of this development is to enable the sitter to induce a trance state to permit the use of his mind and body by the spirit guide. This serves a very useful purpose insofar that the sitter becomes conscious of the personality of the guide and gives the assurance and confidence that what takes place in trance is not the result of any conscious effort on his part.

When the average man or woman is first told, or they become aware, that they may possess the latent gift of healing, it seems too good to be true. Yet they feel very diffident about it and self-conscious, but there is nothing they would like more. So when they become conscious of the nearness or presence of the guide it helps to take away the sense of personal responsibility for the healing and also the self-consciousness—it gives them courage.

The author commenced his healing ministry in this way. It was only after a period of time and the acceptance of the knowledge that the guides are able to work just as well without the need for trance that this was discontinued. I followed out all the traditional practices that I had seen others do. It was only after I had judged these practices in the light of common sense and what I had learned of spirit science that I discarded them one by one. As I commented in the first paragraph of this book, I have learned that the healing act, *as far as the healer is concerned, is one of simplicity.*

On many occasions people have told me how, when they were with a sick person, they had been impressed to place their hands upon the affected part, and as a consequence the pains and symptoms of the trouble vanished. They have been so impressed by these acts that they inquire how they can learn to heal. If they but knew it, there was little for them to learn. The position is that, being human, we are not content to accept the simplicity of healing but want to do something more ourselves.

Every healing is an intelligent act from Spirit. Therefore it is not possible for any technique we adopt to assist this. The healing forces come *through us,* they are not *of us.*

The beginner should not concern himself in the early stages with the individuality of his healing guides—that will come later. He should retire to a room where he can be quiet and undisturbed for say thirty minutes. The period can be extended as time goes on. In the beginning two or three times a week will suffice.

He should make himself comfortable. A Windsor armchair is ideal for this purpose. He has the chair-arms to rest his arms on to facilitate complete relaxation of the body.

The light should be dimmed. A low light prevents the optic nerves being strongly impressed and so disturbing the consciousness. For this reason a blue light can be used. There is no reason for a red light for this character of development unless the sitter wishes it.

The word "concentration" is commonly used in association with psychic development. This is a word of the worst meaning to employ. It is not a mental concentration that is needed but mental abandonment. One should not try to make the mind a blank, for this is not possible.

The ideal to be arrived at is a stage of gentle meditation, with the directive of seeking contact with Spirit. As the physical mind surrenders itself to this and the spirit mind becomes ascendant, so the guide will begin to be able to influence the thought impressions. The mind should dwell upon the desire to heal the sick; to take away pain and remove the causes of disease; to contemplate spiritual ideals. There is no harm in letting the mind play with these ideas, knowing that as thoughts dwell upon these matters they can be helped intuitively from the spirit mind.

The meditation should not be sustained for too long or the mind will become tense. For a change let the mind contemplate beautiful things. Take a mental holiday into a garden of beauty. Float in your imagination down a peaceful river. Let your mind dwell on the idealism portrayed in the scriptures. These are only suggestions but they indicate the way to free the physical mind from the prosaic things in everyday life, thus allowing the spirit mind to assume a superior ascendancy.

It is unlikely, at first, that any difference will be felt within one's self. This is not sitting for trance; to do so would be very unwise. One should never sit solo for this but only in a well-conducted developing circle. The purpose is for meditation and, through this means, for the mind to attune to Spirit, which is very different from sitting to attract spirit people to you.

The first thoughts on each occasion should be prayerful ones addressed to God, the Father of all mankind. Set prayers are of little use for they become mechanical recitations. Simple thoughts are best, in a natural way, as if you are speaking to God. Avoid high-sounding phrases and unnatural ones. Express in these thoughts that you desire to serve Him for all that is good and perfect; to remove disharmony and evil whether it be of the mind or the flesh. Ask that His ministers in Spirit will give you guidance and protection while you meditate and then have the utmost confidence that only good influences will be with you.

Have no fear of any kind in the mind. If one is fearful do not continue.

My colleagues and I never seek attunement with any particular healing guide. We know they are present, so we attune to the spirit realm. The reason for this is that if we limit our attunement with only one spirit personality whatever healing that can take place must be restricted to the wisdom of that one guide. If attunement is sought with the spirit realm then the intelligence which is best able to deal with the problem will "listen in."

After the meditation has been taking place for a while, consider a relative or a friend who is unwell. You will probably know the character of the symptoms of the illness. If you do, then spend a few moments allowing your mind to picture the patient, dwelling on his personality, and the nature of the distress. Meanwhile, let it be done as if you are telling your thoughts to someone who is "listening in" to you. Let it be simple and natural. Do not stress the situation by fervently imploring the spirit to heal him. This only stresses the mind, creates confusion and ends the attunement. Do not dwell upon the condition too long, for this will only succeed in occupying the mind with your own thoughts and again end the attunement. Simply try to project the picture outwards for the guide to receive it. As this is done though your spirit mind, so it will be received by the spirit guide or those who are in association with you on the other side of life. Then follow this up with the gentle request that those who are listening in may be able to take away the pain, to ease the stiffness, relieve the stress, or whatever it may be, so that comfort and perfection may return to the sick one.

Do not try to do too much at first or prolong each situation. After the intercessions for the sick, let the mind continue its relaxation. Hum a favourite hymn tune and so lead the mind back to the return of normal activity, concluding with a prayer of thanks to God.

There is a condition of mind that everyone knows as "day dreaming" when thoughts are wandering, oblivious of other things. This is an illustration of the state of mind to be arrived at during the meditative contemplation.

There is no set time as to how long a sitting should continue. At first, the minutes will seem long ones, but as the sittings continue the time so spent will become a real pleasure and will soon pass.

Avoid fixing a definite time to start the sittings. It is much better to let them take place after the daily tasks have been comfortably finished. Do not hurry these, but rather see happiness in their accomplishment. When you feel the desire to sit for communion with the spirit people that is the right time.

Do not impose upon yourself any penances, such as fastings, etc., before sitting. The body should be comfortable to help relaxation to come in an easy and natural way.

There is an important ideal to be woven into the way of life, and that is to seek to live by a code of true values. You will do no harm to anyone, you will always seek to serve. You will be tolerant and generous in all things. You will not allow temper, ill will, or thoughts of revenge to follow an act that has displeased you. Help your neighbours and friends by acts of kindness, especially those who are sick and lonely and need a word of comfort or an errand undertaken. If during the day you see a sufferer, retain the healing need in reserve in your mind, so that later, in the quietness, you can ask help for him.

These are some of the principles on which absent healing is based. While you cannot promise yourself (or the patients) that any healing result will be seen, it may be that even from the days of your first intercession you will observe the sufferers getting well far more quickly than might otherwise have been expected.

Some people will be able to establish communication with Spirit more quickly than others. No time can be laid down as necessary for development. Each person is a law unto himself and, in fact, development is never finished. It should, however, be seen as the practice of sitting is continued and experience gained, the act of attunement will become easier and eventually become as "second nature", permitting the healer to attune with Spirit as easily as holding a normal conversation with a friend. Moreover, the beginner will be assisting his own spiritual progress.

The next phase of development is the encouraging of the self to receive cosmic strength through characterised breathing. The beginner should sit for a while as described. Then when he establishes peace within, he should become consciously aware of his breathing.

It has already been pointed out in "cosmic healing" that we are surrounded by cosmic forces that are there for our good. We can absorb them directively. To do this successfully one must have the confidence that they exist. The sitter is asked to inhale gently and slowly through the nose, filling the lungs. As the inhalations are made, the sitter will feel that he is drawing into himself inner strength and vitality to supply his body with cleansing and invigorating forces. As he exhales, he should have the consciousness of exuding waste.

The normal healthy body absorbs a blending of all the cosmic forces necessary to maintain a good health balance, but by characterising the inhalations one is purposefully able to strengthen and invigorate oneself and to fill up the reservoir of inner strength.

This practice need not be limited to the periods when sitting for attunement. It can profitably take place at any time of the day; before or on rising, when going out to business or shopping, and again on retiring before sleep comes. As this is practised one will experience that inner feeling of exhilaration, of being "on top of the world."

We are now approaching the time when contact healing can be given. There is no greater joy than the realisation that a patient's pain is being removed or to feel the alignment of a malformation or the dispersal of a growth.

Writing personally, there is no greater joy than the moment of knowing that a beneficial result has taken place, and not even years of healing has diminished this. It may be, for example, that I am dealing with a shoulder joint that has become locked by arthritic adhesions and the patient has not been able to lift the arm sufficiently to comb the hair. With one hand encompassing the joint, looseness of movement is very gently sought by seeking movement with my other hand moving the arm. At first the resistance is felt, the orbit of movement is very small. Then gradually more movement comes, until the arm can swing freely and I intuitively know that the joint has become quite free, so much so that, at times, the arm will at once ascend vertically. This is the moment of sublime happiness for the healer. On other occasions, following my intuitive impressions, I will seek the arm to ascend very gently, to allow for the muscles and tendons to yield to the new movement. Once it is attained, complete looseness generally follows so that the patient can swing the arm in all directions.

It is noteworthy that with the healing of very painful conditions, such as arthritis, usually no pain is caused. If on rare occasions the patient feels pain, then I know that I am moving the limb more than I should and I wait a while for the further healing to take place. This almost complete absence of pain in the healing of stressful conditions is further evidence of the powers of the guides to remove obstructions, etc., painlessly in the ways known to them. When a patient with a locked joint has a forceful manipulation by a doctor, he is given an anaesthetic at first to render him unconscious, but with spirit healing there is no pain.

The only way to prove one's gift is to put it to the test, and confidence will come as the healings are seen to take place. The beginner is most likely to feel very self-conscious in his first efforts, but there must come the time for the "breaking of the ice" and any undue hesitation should be overcome. The healer should be confident within himself and master of the situation. All limiting thoughts and those of "inferiority" should be renounced.

Many healers stand to do their work behind the seated patient. There is no reason for this. As the healer needs to be relaxed to attain attunement, this is far more easily obtained seated in front of the patient.

The healer prepares for attunement. He forgets his surroundings, everything, as he allows his spirit-self to become ascendant, for which his previous sittings have prepared him. As this comes so will he also blend with the patient. A good way to help is to hold the patient's hands and so bring about a sense of "oneness" between them.

At first, the healer can talk freely for a while with his patient, to help him to relax. The patient can be asked to give an account of his troubles and history of his sufferings. This will provide the healer with a picture which the guide will also receive. Oft-times it will help the patient to talk about his condition and feel the sym-

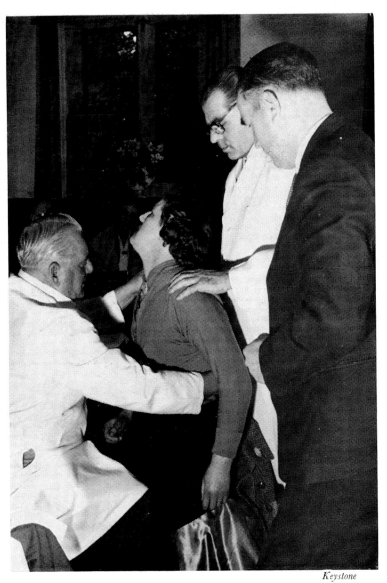

Freeing a locked spine without pain

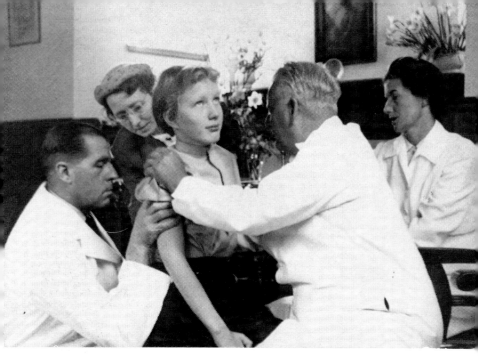

Healing of polio-myelitis in the Sanctuary

Doctors observe the freeing of the joints of a spastic child

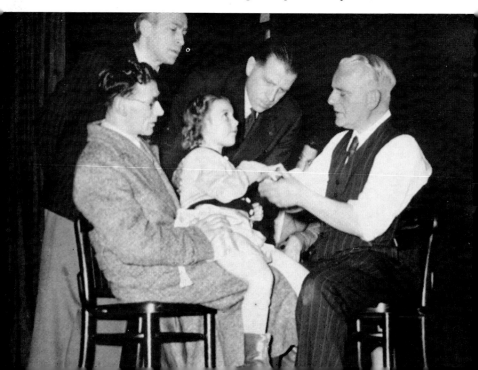

pathy of the healer. As the talking takes place, the healer will learn how to be able to listen and at the same time, through his compassion, permit oneness to be strengthened between his spirit-self and that of the sufferer. It may be helpful if the healer closes his eyes during this time.

It is essential for the patient to be relaxed physically and mentally, to let the body go limp and the mind be at ease. This may be aided by the healer speaking in a soothing and calming voice and by gently passing his hands over the visitor's forehead and head and, if necessary, down the body, with the thought directive that a state of peacefulness may come to the patient.

If a limb is being healed, let it be bent, relaxed and free from muscular tension. Do not attempt to heal if the limb is "pulling" or tensed, but wait until relaxation comes.

As the blending of the healer with his patient takes place there will also come the state of attunement with the healing guide.

The healer may then place one hand over the affected part, his other hand still maintaining contact with the patient as is convenient. Then, for a moment or two, the healer's whole self, his hands, mind and consciousness are welded, as it were, to the patient, that in those moments the healing forces may reach him and bring benefit. These are the important moments. The healer's whole concern is centred on the purpose, with no other thought than that of the healing to be done. He forgets himself. The only "live" thing is his hand, which becomes an "extension" of his mind, and into this he puts his whole being, his very self. This will be done easily and naturally. The hand stays over the affected part for such time as the healer is impressed it is necessary.

The hand may move as if dispersing matter or easing pain, for this is a natural expression of the desire, being but an extension of the mind directive. Whatever the movement the hand may make, let directive thought accompany it. For example, if the trouble is a growth, the fingers should seem to possess the power to dissolve and disperse it. Nothing else matters while this is going on. Maintain sympathetic closeness with the patient, so that for the time being there is only the supreme purpose in view.

4

The time the healing takes need not be of long duration. Healings cannot be forced or more progress made than that which can be received at the time. With stubborn and chronic conditions a number of healing treatments is necessary. If the healer does not see all the easement come that he would wish for, he should avoid carrying on and trying to do it himself.

As the healer commences his work, he may feel or sense that one hand is more positively used than the other. This is called the power hand, and should be used over the affected part. A further explanation of this is that the healer feels power flow through his arm and hand. A "vibration" may be experienced through it, or a feeling of heat or cold.

The vibration is an effect and is not healing. The heat and cold are not clinical, and their presence should give the beginner that comfort and assurance that he is being used as a channel for healing.

As with all other things, it is experience that counts; experience by the guide in the use of his human instrument; experience by the healer in being used and how to blend with the patient. If the healer does not see all the progress made at one time that he would wish for, he should not blame himself or the patient or the guide. He must be content with knowing that the maximum good has been given for the time being and to look for the coming of further relief next time.

No healing can take place unless the cause is first removed. It may well be that a little time is needed for this purpose, especially if the primary cause lies in some form of mind or inner-self disharmony. If there is muscular wastage, as in some cases of paralysis, time is again needed to rebuild the weakened tissues.

The healer should leave his mind free to follow the impressions that are intuitively given by the guide. Often he will receive advice to be passed on to the patient to show how he can help himself to take advantage of the progressive benefits the healing brings.

CHAPTER SIX

HEALING AND THE CHURCH

If it is true that the Christian Church desires to recover its lost gift of healing, then all it needs is the services of healer-priests to put the wish into effect.

It is pertinent to recall that with the Spiritualist and Christian Science religions, spiritual healing forms an integral part of their work. Therefore they set out to develop the gift of healing with those of their members who may possess the healing potential. That they succeed is proven by the Spiritualist healers and Christian Science practitioners who are numbered by the thousand. It may be truly said that the strength of the Christian Science movement has been built upon the testimonies of the healed. With Spiritualism, its ever-growing status is the outcome of the proof of survival as given by clairvoyants, spirit healing and other forms of communication through mediumship.

Why is it then, that with the Protestant and Roman Catholic religions they do not encourage the development of the faculty of healing with their priests? If the Pope can be the means of securing only three supernormal healings in his lifetime, he will become eligible for sainthood when he passes into spirit life.

Every year many thousands of pilgrims, crippled, infirm and suffering from all manner of diseases, travel to Lourdes. They go full of faith in the belief they will be cured. They receive the prayerful support of Cardinals and innumerable priests. There are daily processions and continuous church services. If faith alone could cure disease, then these conditions for spiritual healing should be ideal.

Every case of healing at Lourdes is subject to the closest scrutiny by a combined church and medical panel, which is as it should be. Nineteen hundred and fifty eight celebrated the centenary of the pilgrimages. Yet only fifty-four cases of healing have been approved by the panel in the hundred years. In view of the hundreds of thousands, possibly millions, of sick people who have made the journey to Lourdes, this result is lamentably insignificant. Most Spiritualist healers of experience claim a better record than this. In my book, *The Evidence for Spiritual Healing,* I cited over ten thousand cases of supernormal healings covering a period of four years. True, these cases were not subject to any impartial investigation. I would have gladly welcomed one, but, as will be shown later, medical people are most reluctant to do this. It is right to ask: Why is it that with Spiritualist healers there is so much more success than is seen with the fervent organised might of the largest section of the Christian Church—the Roman Catholic?

To this question can be added a further one. The Church of England and all other branches of Christian religion include in their services prayers for the sick. Their priests pay innumerable visits to the afflicted in their homes, where individual prayers are offered for recoveries. While doubtless some healings take place, the percentage of success is very small compared with the total effect. Archbishops, Bishops, and their contemporaries in the Roman Catholic Church, the Pope and the Cardinals, claim to be God's lieutenants and possess the power of audience with Him. This privilege is bestowed upon all priests at their ordination. Then why is it that the Church confesses that it has lost the gift of healing and needs commissions of enquiry to try and find the way to recover it?

Surely the answer is that they have the wrong approach, and Spiritualists and Christian Scientists have a much more effective one.

The attitude of the Church is that healings do not need the intermediaries of those we know as spirit guides, that healing alone comes from the personality of God in acts of direct dispen-

sation in favour of a sick individual, and that these acts are answers
to prayer and faith.

It is a logical assumption that the means by which spiritual
healings are brought about follows the same processes. It is unlikely that there are a different set of rules for the Roman Catholic,
the Anglican Church, the Christian Scientist and the Spiritualist.
The much higher percentage of success seen with the Spiritualist
concept indicates that they are closer to the means through which
healings occur.

Therefore when a healing follows the application of prayer
offered by a minister of any Church, it implies that unknowingly
the application for help has been received in the spirit realm and
the good service of the healing guides has been brought into
being. If this is so, then it supports the contention that when the
Church accepts the principle that the spirit healing personalities
are God's ministers carrying out the divine intention that a far
larger degree of healing success will be seen and the Church will
then recover its lost gift of healing.

This argument not only applies to ministers of religion but to
doctors too. Many doctors can tell of recoveries taking place
that are contrary to their expectations based upon medical knowledge. It is suggested that when a doctor feels compassion for a
patient and inwardly offers a prayer for healing to reach the sick
one, he unconsciously attunes to the spirit realm, linking up with
the healing guides who then help the patient to recover in the ways
known to them.

The Church view is based on the premise that "with God all
things are possible," and presumes that when God wishes He over-
rides the physical and spiritual laws in a favourable discrimination
for a named person. If spirit healings are God's responsibility,
then He is also responsible for non-healing. This means that the
ever-loving and merciful God most often turns a deaf ear to the
prayers of Popes, Archbishops, Cardinals, Bishops and the
priesthood in general. It means that He ignores the heartrending
supplications of parents who watch their little ones die in agony.
It means that, if the Church view is right, God hears our prayers

and that He is conscious of the needs of each one of His children, but He is content to let the sick suffer their pains and live and die in stress.

I do not believe this is the case at all. God is not responsible for our sicknesses; nor does He impose them as punishments upon us. Disease and sickness arise from contravention of the perfect laws that govern creation. They are the outcome of "cause and effect," and we have no right to seek God's omnipotent power to discriminate in favour of any one person.

There is no evidence in the scriptures that when God has work to do He does it Himself; instead, the Bible story tells that He appoints His angels or ministers to accomplish it. Thus we view our healing guides as "priests of God," carrying out the divine plan to subjugate evil and disease.

Many people think that the established and unorthodox religions are mainly concerned with preserving their theologies and the fabric of their organisations, and that they erroneously try to adjust spirit healing to come within these limitations.

Spiritual healing is God's gift to all His people, irrespective of race or creed. He does not provide one set of healing laws for the Spiritualist and another for the Church of England or the Roman Catholic, etc. Spiritual healing can never become the prerogative of any religion or of any man.

It appears that Spiritualism and Christian Science (the healing religions), through their beliefs and their ability to use the gift of healing, have a more correct appreciation of spiritual values and the divine plan.

There is no reason at all why the Churches should not be able to develop healer-priests, if they would but acknowledge the truth of spirit communication and co-operation between the two realms of life.

Archbishop Temple nominated his own committee to report to him whether such communication and co-operation was true. By a majority of eight to three they found it was so. For the reason that the majority report found in favour of Spiritualist beliefs the report was suppressed and never officially published.

There must be many clergymen who have an inner yearning to heal the sick, otherwise they would not have given themselves to their calling. Numbers of them have come to our Sanctuary to develop the gift. One of these was a Congregationalist minister, the Rev. Alex. Holmes, whose church was at Godalming. He attended a number of healing sessions at our Sanctuary, received instruction and co-operated with us in treating the sick. In this way he developed his gift of healing with outstanding success. After a period he sought a wider field for his healing work and courageously accepted the ministry of Cavendish Chapel in Manchester.

This chapel, which seats nearly two thousand people had, at that time, a membership which had fallen to about forty. At the first public healing service at which my colleagues, Mr. and Mrs. Burton, and I officiated, there was not room for all who wished to attend. Mr. Holmes conducted daily personal healing and public healing services once a month. Before long he had four hundred communicants, and thousands of people came to the church for healing and worship. In two years all debts were paid off and there were sufficient funds to have the church renovated.

Mr. Holmes, fired by his healing zeal, trained other ministers to heal. Through his efforts over fifty other Nonconformist churches commenced regular healing services with the consequent building-up of their membership and prestige. Mr. Holmes then went to Canada to continue his mission and has conducted successful healing services in the main cities of that Dominion and in the U.S.A. What he has done others can do. I have given a standing invitation to the Church of England to help the development of the healing gift for a number of their ministers, but this has not yet been accepted.

Not one of the reports of the various commissions has indicated any way whatsoever to show their ministers how they may develop the healing gift. Where suggestions have been made, they are bound up with ritual and mechanical services. They seek to limit the healing to the members of their churches. This was expressed in an editorial in the *Church Times* which said, "If spiritual healing is to proceed on sound lines then it must be kept within the sacramental life of the Church." The report of the Archbishops' Commission on Divine Healing recommended all manner of conditions as being necessary before an effort is made to heal the sick. Any attempt to imprison healing in this fashion is doomed to failure.

I spoke to one parson who used to hold the orthodox healing services in his church, following the prescribed ritual, saying the same mechanical prayer over each patient as he laid his hands on their heads. I said to him: "If one of your people has arthritis in the shoulder, why not place your hands on the shoulder and prayerfully ask for the arthritis to be taken away?" He replied: "I am not allowed to do that—but after the service is over I take the sick into my vestry and there I seek for them *real healing*."

The Church freely admits the existence of evil spirits. Then why not admit the existence of good spirit people, carrying out the divine intention, just as priests are trying to do in this life? The Church says it believes in the communion of saints. Why not seek their aid in a practical way? This is what Spiritualism does in healing, though we term the "saints" as "healing guides."

The Church as a whole should not be unmindful of the growth of public support for spiritual healing. In recent years I have conducted public healing services in the largest halls in every main city in the United Kingdom. These have been all too small to accommodate the great numbers who wished to attend. Perhaps the largest of these was in King's Hall, Belle Vue, Manchester, where seven thousand people attended, with another meeting being held the following year. In London, the Royal Albert Hall has been filled to capacity on two occasions and the Royal Festival Hall on three. The usual story is, especially in the North of England, that without any need for public advertising every seat has been disposed of months before the date of the service. Healing missions have also been held in Cyprus, Greece, Holland and Switzerland. The largest halls were secured and they were filled to overflowing.

The evidence exists that in our country (as shown by the Rev. Alex. Holmes) that when public healing services are held the churches are filled. This is the means to bring people back under the guidance of the Church and so effectively play the part on which it should be engaged, that of spiritualising mankind.

Only silly prejudice is the barrier preventing spiritual healing becoming a part of the pastoral work of the clergy. This barrier is in the word "Spiritualism." Leaders of the Church feel that if they recommend the development of healer-priests on the lines suggested in this book it will imply they are favouring beliefs on which they have poured scorn for several decades. Words and beliefs do not matter. Truth is important.

When priests spend their lives in the service of the Church, helping all those in need of their prayers, they are indeed priests of God. When the time comes for them to pass on, it is only natural that many of them desire to continue to serve God in the ways that are open to them in spirit life. They then see, as the Archbishop's committee on Spiritualism found to be proven, that they can influence for good the minds of those they have left behind. Because they do so they are priests of God in a more exalted way. They do not deserve the opprobrium of being described as "departed spirits," or "disembodied souls" who are evil and lieutenants of the devil.

It is quite natural, too, for doctors who have the love of their profession at heart to wish to continue to serve and help the sick of this world, particularly as there can be no organic disease in the greater life.

This is the truth that the Church must acknowledge. It cannot turn a blind eye for all time to the demonstrable proof of spirit healing and the part that the guides (who surely are priests of God) so willingly play in furthering the divine plan.

Each report from the various Church commissions expresses the opinion that public healing services in churches is undesirable. It is said that such services are likely to create emotional hysteria, and to give the sick a false sense of faith. It is true that healing services are emotional, but there is nothing wrong in that. After all, the parson in the pulpit is a dull fellow if he cannot speak from the heart with some emotion and arouse emotional feelings in his

congregation. This is quite different from hysteria. In all the many
large public healing services that I have held there has never been
any evidence of hysteria. Surely there is no reason to suppose that
a Church healing service held with dignity would become
hysterical. In the U.S.A. there are some types of evangelist healers
who purposely set out to create a tense atmosphere which has led
to hysterical outbursts. But that should not happen here. After all
Christ conducted His healing in public places before the multitude.
To-day there is no real reason why it would not be good for people
to go to church to be healed or to give their sympathy and help for
others to be healed.

All the reports have adopted the superior attitude that Spiritualist healings concern only the welfare of the body and that the
Church is more concerned with healing the total man, body and
soul. No healing can take place until the cause has been overcome.
We know that as the origin of most sicknesses arise in some form
of mind or soul disharmony, then obviously our healing must
embrace the healing of the soul. We often hear that with spirit
healing the character of a man or woman will change for the better;
the sadistic and cruel husband will become loving and temperate,
the alcoholic will give up drink, etc. This is surely healing of the
soul.

The reports, in advancing the idea that the Church is more concerned with healing the soul than the body, advocate the necessity
of preparing the patient before he receives healing by first giving
him a period of religious instruction. The Church of England
report is very definite on this point. It is suggested that as a condition of healing the sick one must first turn to God, confess his
sins and take holy communion, and that the priest should not
seek healing until he is confident that the sufferer is truly penitent.
This is surely a wrong attitude. It is best to heal the sick person
first and to preach to him afterwards. It is indeed cruel to subject
a man or woman who is in pain to a series of lectures on godliness
as a preliminary to easing his or her suffering. It is when the
sufferer has seen his troubles healed through spiritual healing that
he will be more receptive to preaching. He will have had the

demonstration of the divine intention by seeing his pains and troubles taken away. Besides, the patient may die while he is being "preached at".

The Church commits an error in attempting to separate healing into divisions. *All* healing is divine. To try and divide this into body healing and soul healing can only lead to failure.

Another error the reports show is the suggestion that with each denomination the healing is to be limited to church members. Priests are told they will be justified in refusing healing to an outsider. It seems to be necessary to remind Church leaders of the parable of the Good Samaritan. Christ did not catechise the leper and the cripple before He healed them. No priest of God should limit his healing in this way.

At our Sanctuary we see people of all religious beliefs, and of none, healed. Hindus have come with their caste insignia on their foreheads. We have healed the Mohammedan, the Jew and the agnostic. All are God's children and the gift of healing is open to everybody.

When the Church modernises its ancient theology and accepts the truth that its own commission found, that life is continuous, that spirit communication is real, and that healing is God's plan to demonstrate in this scientific age that man is a spiritual being, we shall see its influence restored. Thus it would lead the way for mankind to accept a new code of values that will outlaw all the ignoble trends in human conduct to-day.

CHAPTER SEVEN

HEALING AND THE MEDICAL PROFESSION

One can perhaps understand the reluctance of members of the medical profession, from personal motives, to admit that others who are not registered practitioners can heal the sick. Yet it is pleasing to note that there is an increasing tendency with individual medical men to acknowledge the efficacy of spiritual healing.

In the past year I received over one thousand letters from doctors asking for healing for themselves, their families and patients. Many of them have come to the Sanctuary for personal healing or have brought patients for our treatment.

All this has had to be done in secrecy, for if the General Medical Council became aware of their actions they would be liable to disciplinary action with the possibility of being struck off the medical register and having their livelihood taken away from them.

Other good signs are that an increasing number of hospital doctors are sending patients to us and medical staffs have invited us to treat patients in the hospitals, but officially the ban on co-operation continues.

It is also noteworthy that when the British Medical Association has been asked by other influential bodies to express an opinion upon spiritual healing, it has been admitted that through this means "healings apparently take place that cannot be explained by medical science."

In the past whenever we have asked the British Medical Association or eminent physicians to investigate and comment upon a supernormal healing, they have either refused to do so or have given replies such as "mistaken diagnosis", "remission", "spontaneous healing", "too much time has elapsed", or the contrary, "show us this patient in five years' time", "X-ray plates have been wrongly labelled", etc.

An example of this sort of thing was the case of a man who was diagnosed by two specialists as suffering from a malignant cancer of the throat. A small section of flesh was taken from the throat for a biopsy (laboratory examination) when the cancerous state was confirmed. An operation was said to be essential and this was arranged to be done two weeks later. The same day that the biopsy confirmed the cancer we were informed of the condition and asked to give absent healing. Before the two weeks were over, the throat swellings had disappeared, as well as the hoarseness of the voice and the man felt well in every way. He then requested, on our advice, a further examination. After this had been made by the same two specialists, they declared that the cancerous condition no longer existed. This case was submitted to a doctor (who was investigating spiritual healing) for his consideration. He wrote to the specialists, explaining the intervention of spiritual healing and asked if they would acknowledge a cure by this means or supply an alternative explanation.

The reply from the specialists was, "By a fortunate coincidence the small segment of tissue taken for the biopsy just happened to contain all the cancer." This story with the explanation was printed in the *British Medical Journal* to support the view that spiritual healing was unproven.

This attitude may be exemplified by my experience with the Archbishops' Commission on Divine Healing. Before I gave evidence in person I was asked to supply six cases of supernormal healing. Instead of six I gave over seventy; all recent cases that could easily be checked. When I appeared before the Commission a doctor, nominated by the British Medical Association, held up these medical histories which I had supplied and then put them down saying, "These could all be spontaneous healings." (Spontaneous healings means that nature has in some not understood way asserted itself to overcome the disease.) When I pointed out to the doctor that the cases submitted were all in the category of "incurables" and therefore spontaneous healing could not reasonably be applied to them, his reply was, "Too many doctors are saying people are incurable when they are not."

Later, at the Commission's request, I submitted eight detailed histories of patients suffering from so-called incurable diseases in which complete recoveries had taken place. A special committee of the British Medical Association was appointed to investigate these. This committee did not interview any of the patients or call for any hospital report. I will give one example. A boy of three contracted an undiagnosable disease. He could not assimilate any food, and developed the symptom of paralysis. He was bent over and swayed from side to side like a pendulum. For seven years he was an inmate of a number of hospitals. Various treatments were tried without avail. Many specialists considered his case and all declared the disease was incurable. The boy was brought down to a London hospital for children and was placed under the care of an eminent physician,* who told the father, "There is nothing that we can do for him." So he was sent home, totally incurable with no further medical treatment to be given. By this time the boy had degenerated into a terrible state. He was a living skeleton, partially paralysed and still swaying like a pendulum.

The boy's sister wrote to me for absent healing and this was given. In three weeks the swaying ceased, he was taking nourishment and before long was able to go to school, a perfectly healthy and normal boy. He is now sixteen years of age and has passed his general education examinations. For the last six years his health has been so perfect that he has not needed a doctor. It should be mentioned that when this case was submitted to the Commission the boy was about twelve years old.

The medical committee disposed of this case simply. It said, "As this boy is not now under a doctor, no investigation can be made." One might think that such a case as this provided a challenge to the medical committee—they only needed to send to the hospital concerned for the boy's medical history, to confirm or

---

* The names of the hospitals and the doctors concerned in these reports are available to any bona fide enquirer.

deny the accuracy of the healing. It seems clear to me that if this committee had made a full investigation they would have been compelled to acknowledge the efficacy of spirit healing.

Spiritual healers are not opposed in any way to medical men; on the contrary they seek co-operation. It is common sense to avail ourselves of the wisdom that man has attained in the medical field and take advantage of it. It is as foolish for a person to say, "I won't go to a doctor," as it is for a doctor to say, "Spirit healing is a myth." The ideal method of combating disease is to obtain co-operation between the two methods of treatment. They are complementary to each other.

Medical treatment can do little for those patients where the primary cause for the sickness lies in mind and inner-self disharmony; in this spirit healing can be of great assistance.

Often we hear it said of a patient receiving spiritual healing, "He is the hospital's prize patient," or "The doctors cannot understand where he gets his strength from," or "The doctors are amazed and say he is a miracle." Yet when we ask, "Have the doctors been informed he is receiving spiritual healing?" the reply comes, "No, we were afraid to tell them for fear of what they might say." I have known cases where doctors have refused to treat patients who have been receiving absent healing from us.

Spiritual healers have at times been able to indicate the causes of disease resulting from their experience and from information given to them from the spirit world. In 1945, I submitted that the basic cause behind most forms of skin disease lay in nervous tensions and frustrations and that ointments, etc., were not curative. In 1947, this was claimed as a great medical discovery. Similarly spiritual healers have long known that the origin of organic diseases most often lay in inner-self disharmonies. It is only in recent years that this truth has been generally accepted. So it is with cancer. Four years ago I published the statement that most forms of cancer, especially breast cancers in women, resulted from frustrations and inner-self unrest. Now we see eminent physicians like Sir Heneage Ogilvie expressing similar views, saying, "A happy man never gets cancer." Being impressed by Sir Heneage's advanced outlook on the subject of cancer, and feeling that he would acknowledge the spirit healing factor if he thought a cure was due to it, I wrote to him. I asked him if he would investigate some cures of patients by spiritual healing who had been medically declared to have incurable cancers. I supplied him with a specimen case history of one healing. In his reply Sir Heneage indicated that he would not be satisfied with other medical opinions and would concern himself only with cases that had been under his jurisdiction.

Leukemia, or cancer of the blood, is another disease totally incurable in medical opinion, yet to-day we are seeing a measure of success in healing it. On one occasion, a boy in a Midland hospital made such a sensational recovery, for the time being, following absent healing, that he was held up to be an exhibition case. I wrote to the professor in charge and suggested that in view of this abnormal recovery, dated by the commencement of spiritual healing, he might consider letting me know of any other serious cases that came under his care so that we could co-operate with absent healing in a similar way. I also sent a copy of the invitation to the British Medical Association, but received no reply from either.

It is a matter of history that the medical profession has always, at first, opposed new measures and new ideas. Only in recent times has it agreed that certain patients can benefit from hypnotism; before this it was adamant in its condemnation. Similarly it opposed the introduction of the hygenic methods advanced by Lord Lister and the use of anæsthetics.

While it is true that minor ailments and more serious disease in their early stages yield readily to spirit healing, it is not the wish of healers to supplant the doctor, although it may be thought good to ease the burden of the overworked general practitioner and to lighten the demands now being made on the all too inadequate hospital accommodation.

On one occasion I was invited to demonstrate spirit healing before a number of doctors belonging to a medical society in Wimpole Street. I asked them to bring their own patients, which they did. At first the doctors did not appear to me to be very interested as they sat in lounge chairs all around the large room. The first

Healing scene at the Royal Festival Hall

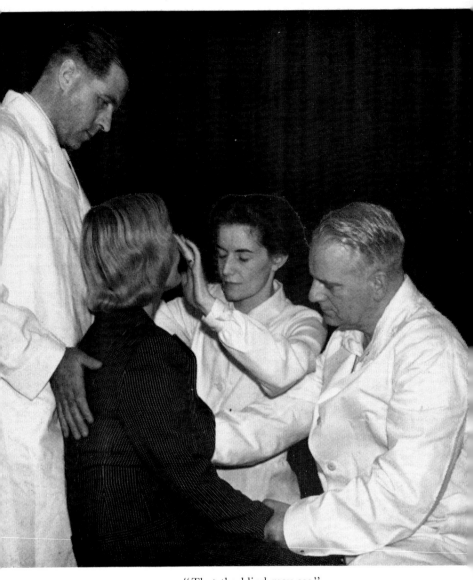

"That the blind may see"

patient was a woman suffering from disseminated sclerosis. She was helped into the room by two friends, for the paralysis had taken away her balance and power of controlled leg movements. I explained the healing purpose to the doctors as, firstly, mobility was restored to the spastic spine and then said how the co-ordination for leg movements would come. This patient responded very well. She was able to stand upright and walk reasonably well with her hand on the arm of a friend. This first healing so impressed the doctors that with all the remaining patients they stood up, crowding round to observe closely how the beneficial changes took place with freeing arthritic joints and spinal re-adjustments, etc. The occasion ended with the doctors asking me to give them healing treatment for their own troubles!

At public healing meetings I often ask if there is a doctor present who would like to come up and verify the ill-condition with the patient and to check closely the healing result. Almost on every occasion this has taken place the doctor has signified his agreement that the trouble has been overcome. The only occasion I recall where a doctor refused to give this acknowledgment was for the reason that he would need to see the patient stripped before he would give his testimony. At one of these meetings, held in Glasgow, at which the Lord Provost was present, it was the Medical Officer of Health for the city who freely expressed his acceptance of the healing results.

When doctors come to the Sanctuary, I invite them to co-operate with the healing. For example, should I have a patient with a "poker spine," the doctor is first invited to check the severity of the condition. Then I ask him to place his fingers with mine on the patient's spine to note, as the healing treatment proceeds, the coming of mobility to the vertebrae. Next I request him to check that the spine has become completely free, by bending, bowing, arching, rotating it and so on. One doctor told us that he would gladly give up five years of his life to be able to achieve what we were able to do through spiritual healing.

It may well be that those doctors who have a real love of their profession and view their patients as "people" and not just "cases" are, at times, the subconscious channel through whom the spirit healing forces flow. It is the doctors more than the parsons who observe supernormal healings take place as they sit by the bedside, hold the patient's hands and silently, offer a prayer for the sufferer to be made well. In discussions and in print many of the stories of such unexpected healings have been told by doctors. If all the evidence of such healings could be collated it would surprise the British Medical Association. In this connection there is need to differentiate between the doctor who *feels* for his patients as opposed to the one whose interest is purely professional, which leads to the telling of a story.

An ardent Spiritualist, discussing survival with her doctor, said to him, "When you pass on, will you go on healing the sick?" His reply was, "Heaven forbid!" He was just a professional doctor.

Is it not reasonable to assume that with those doctors who possess that love of healing and compassion for the sick, when the time comes for them to enter into spirit life they are pleased to further their studies and eventually become healing guides?

While the British Medical Association will not officially recognise spiritual healing through a Spiritualist, it has established official liaison with the Church on this subject. The Association welcomes discussion and co-operation with their members and the clergy in their respective districts. From this co-operation there has been, as yet, no evidence printed or acknowledged in the medical journals or in the reports of any of the Church Commissions of Enquiry to indicate any practical result. The reason is not hard to seek. It is simply that the Church has lost the gift of healing it possessed in its early years and doctors are co-operating with those who are not healers.

If the British Medical Association would only extend similar facilities to Spiritualist healers who are achieving good results, what a different story might be told. Healers would welcome co-operation, for it is felt that the ideal form of treatment for difficult conditions is medical treatment plus healing. While they are complementary to each other, it should be kept in mind that the processes are entirely different. Medical treatment is the use of physical medicines and other therapies, while spiritual healing comes from another dimension altogether—that of Spirit.

It may be that, with some patients, spiritual healing would play the major part. In arthritis, when the cause had been mastered and the joints loosened, physiotherapy, etc., would assist the patient to further progress. In other cases the medical treatment may be of the greater importance and the spiritual healing play its supporting role in giving strength and soothing mind and nerve tensions.

Of recent times, in discussion between doctors and the clergy, some anxiety has been expressed lest the priests, through the part they play, obtain the credit instead of the doctors. The result could be that the sick would be more likely to go to the priest than the doctor. Arising from all this the ruling has been accepted that the priest must always play second fiddle to the doctor.

Spiritual healers carry on their work inspired by love of their fellows. They are not primarily concerned who gets the credit, but that the sick should be made well. At the same time, when co-operation between healers and doctors comes, as it must, there must be no question of which is subordinate to the other or argument as to where any credit is due, otherwise the act of co-operation will become abortive.

With the progressive recognition of the healing potential throughout the medical profession (after all, it is the general practitioner who is able to observe its good results when he gains the friendship and confidence of his patients who confide in him and tell about the help they have received from spiritual healing) we shall see the day when the British Medical Association will take the trouble sympathetically to conduct a *bona-fide* investigation into healing. From this may arise that degree of co-operation we wish to see; to lessen the burden of sickness, prevent its coming, and give a full purpose in life to those who may otherwise die before their full time.

CHAPTER EIGHT

THE DIVINE PURPOSE

An agnostic said to me: "I grant that you have some power to heal the sick, but when you do heal an individual person and take away the pain or disease, what is the purpose of it? To make one person better amid the millions who are sick is an insignificant thing". I replied that, while the healing of, say, Mrs. Brown in Bournemouth is a tremendous thing for her and her family, so that happiness replaces sorrow, it is not so important in the full scheme of things. It is the implications arising from the healing that are important.

When a sufferer is deemed to be incurable and is rejected by the medical profession any further treatment can only be a waste of time, he is told. Thereafter he has to be content with "tablets" from his local doctor to ease the pain. When, as frequently happens, such an "incurable" is cured, it should make him and all those around him acknowledge a demonstration of spirit power. It should prove to all concerned that an unearthly power and intelligence have intervened. Through the accumulation of a great mass of supporting evidence—through Spiritualism—it is proved that this intelligence and power come from highly evolved individuals in spirit life.

The thinking man will know that nothing in physical life can be receptive to any process or force unless there exists the ability to receive it. Some metals are good conductors of electricity, others are not. Radio and television incorporate the transfer and reception of characterised energies. The components of radio and television are arranged in such qualitative attunement that they are sensitive to the energy variations.

So it is with the human being. There exists within him a qualitative faculty that permits him to receive healing forces transmitted by a spirit intelligence. Therefore within his total make-up there must be faculties that are receptive to Spirit, and he must possess a spirit body that is functioning now.

Let us consider what takes place in a large hall where healing is being publicly demonstrated. There are thousands of unseen forces and vibrations, light and sound radiations, electrical impulses and numbers of radionic waves, etc. It only needs the introduction of an attuned instrument, like a radio, to give the evidence of their existence.

At the public healing demonstration the spirit guides are present, and their attuned instruments, the healers. When a patient comes to the platform suffering, shall we assume, from arthritis, with locked joints, the guides direct through the healer the necessary and exact quality of dispersing force to break up the adhesions and allow normal movement to return. The healing of such arthritic troubles has been witnessed thousands of times. It is not just a coincidence. The sufferer may have had a locked joint for a number of years. No amount of suggestion or will-power can free it—otherwise one assumes the doctors would have freed the joint in this way.

There is only one solution. The joint cannot move while the arthritic adhesions cement it into immobility. The obstacles that prevent the movement must be removed. No one can open a door that is screwed up. The screws must first be removed for the door to open. To free an arthritic joint in a few moments, sometimes in no measurable time at all, indicates that the intelligence behind the planned effort has administered the characterised particular force to break up the atomic formations of the obstacles, returning them to their primal states. This is accomplished without harming any of the adjacent tissue, and without any pain at all.

Thus to return to my argument. The patient must have been in harmony with the healing directive. This could not be unless the patient's body was receptive to spirit forces.

These explanations are a prelude to the full answer my agnostic friend needs. Observers of world history acknowledge that divine intervention takes place in times of need. This explains the coming of all the prophets, Confucius, Mohammed and Christ, and other leaders of good thought like Wilberforce and Wesley, to mention two examples. Look at the world conditions when Christ was born. The Roman Empire was showing the early signs of decay, debauchery, cruelty and slavery were prevalent. Politics were decadent. The rule of the sword decided human destiny. Life was of no importance. Leprosy, sickness and disease were everywhere. I need not elaborate any further to show how, through His teachings, miracles and healings, the high concept of Christianity was born.

We read in the olden times how the waters of the Red Sea were parted to enable the Israelites to escape. In more modern times, we wonder why it was that the angry seas, lashed by winds of gale force, suddenly subsided to allow the little boats to bring away the British forces from Dunkirk. We have the evidence of the Angels of Mons, and the inexplicable change of war plans by the enemy when we were in a helpless position. If I am thought to be arrogant in claiming these incidents on behalf of our race, I reply that not only ourselves but the enemy now acknowledges there was right on our side.

So it may be to-day. Spiritual values are at a discount. Youth, materialistic in outlook, has no general belief in religion. The churches are emptying. We are living in a time of scientific achievement. People are no longer willing to accept religion simply because it is preached to them. The sacredness of life is losing its significance and is being valued less and less. There exists world-wide suspicion between nations who feel secure only behind the possession of the hydrogen bomb.

We are all inherently spiritual. Mankind has ever been discontented with his lot—and this is as it should be. Yet behind this there is the idealism for peace and the desire to live in harmony with one's neighbours. Mankind is spiritually hungry, but the old order of "churchianity" does not satisfy him. Thus it may well be that the resurrection of the healing gift in our age is the answer.

As Christ demonstrated the power of the spirit in the miracles and healings, so today we are able to demonstrate the truth that a spiritual heritage lies before us all, the ability to have communication with spirit life and that we must be spiritual beings to become part of the healing process.

The weakness of the Church is that it cannot demonstrate to the questing mind the proof of an individual soul and a hereafter. The strength of spiritual healing is that it does furnish this proof.

This was the answer I gave the agnostic. It has been shown, over and over again, that an agnostic is the most easily converted to the truth of spiritual healing for, as a rule, he possesses a reasoning mind. It is not so easy to convert a man of religion, for he has prejudice against Spiritualism.

We often hear that people who have attended healing sessions and public healing demonstrations have a new and spiritual outlook on life, and that they pray to God for the first time since they were children.

We do not believe that the healing of the sick is the whole of the divine plan. Apart from its leading mankind to accept a new code of spiritual values to overcome the present materialistic ones, it has a further purpose, not only to heal, but to prevent disease.

Surely it is obvious that if eighty per cent. of physical disease has its origin in forms of mind and inner-self disharmonies, then the cultivation of a higher spiritual outlook of life must of necessity lessen the cause of disease. As the two realms of life become more closely interwoven, and healing becomes as second nature, enabling us to respond naturally to spiritual directives, so must the toll of disease be progressively overcome.

I look for the day when confidence through experience will bring healing into every home, and disabilities will yield as they arise. The parent will seek the help of the unseen spirit people for their children and dear ones in the same way that they use homely remedies to-day.

PART TWO

THE APPLICATION OF SPIRITUAL HEALING

CHAPTER NINE

HEALING FORCES

There is no such thing as a miracle. Many healings seem to be miraculous because we have not been able to comprehend the manner of their performance. As we are more able to understand the character of the healing forces so the "miracle" is changed into a reasoned result.

We know that all matter is energy and composed of atoms. Each atomic element is constructed of energy in a precise form. As one atom is associated with another so it is influenced and a new substance is formed. Scientists are now able to break up the ordered formation of an atom and liberate the energies of which it is constructed.

The human body, and every one of the uncountable number of living cells of which it is composed, is atomic. When cells become diseased it means that there is a wrong association with some other form of energy, or that they are not receiving the right quota of nourishment, or senile conditions are settling in and their good purpose is frustrated.

The healing of organic troubles implies that a chemical change takes place. This doctors seek by giving medicines and treatments that promote a beneficial chemical change in the functioning of the bodily systems and influence cellular health.

Spirit healing is an extension of this practice in principle but in a far more advanced and precise way.

The precise manner in which this is attained is conjectural, but certain conclusions can be drawn from established facts. For example, there are many cases on record where a substantial growth has disappeared in a short time by both contact and absent healing methods. It is a common experience in contact healing to see a prominent goitre appreciably decrease in size and, at times, to vanish completely under the healer's fingers. This has been publicly demonstrated on scores of occasions.

X-ray plates have shown the presence of stones in the gall bladder and kidneys. After the intervention of spirit healing further X-ray photographs show they are no longer there. Tumours, fibroid growths and cancers have been pathologically proved to exist. They have been recorded on X-ray plates. They have been visually observed when a patient's body has been opened for investigation. Yet following the healing directive they have disappeared.

I recall one case of a man who was operated upon and the surgeon found an advanced cancer that was inoperable. The patient was sewn up and sent home to die. Absent healing was asked for and given. The painful symptoms disappeared. The man regained his vitality and put on weight. It so happened that a year later he again had cause for a surgical operation for prostate trouble. He was operated on by the same surgeon as on the previous occasion. The surgeon was aware of the man's medical history, and looked for the cancer of which he could find no trace. He was so surprised that he claimed it could not possibly be the same man.

Reference has already been made to the ease with which arthritic calcifications cementing joints into a locked state have been removed. Another phase of dispersal that can also be mentioned here is the dissolution of thrombosis.

Thus we are faced with the situation that substances that have been proved to exist disappear with healing, contrary to all medical knowledge and expectation. The conclusion can thus be drawn that through the healing effort the guides have been able to direct a dispersing form of energy that has broken up the atomic formation of the substance.

The whole of the healing story provides abundant evidence of the superior wisdom of the spirit guides. If man to-day, with the use of heavy and elaborate processes, is able to split the atom, then is it beyond credence that the guides can use their advanced knowledge to do something similar in a much more simple and natural way?

It is obvious that different forms of energies are needed for differing states. For example, a different character of force would be required to disperse a gall-stone than that needed to disperse a goitre.

Supporting evidence for this thesis is provided by the act of "apporting" as witnessed with physical mediumship. Apporting means the bringing of an object from a distance without any physical means. I have seen this occur a number of times. On one occasion, in reasonable light, an object was brought into a room where some friends and I were sitting and dropped into my hands.* This was an Egyptian amulet made of Thebian glass. Its quality, plus the inscription, dated it as being 3,500 years old. Mediums who possess this gift are able, in daylight, to have objects of various kinds materialise in their hands. Live birds and fishes have also been apported. Consideration of this act implies that the "condition" of the energy of which the article is composed is changed into a non-physical state that renders it impervious to friction in instantaneous travelling through the atmosphere. Then it has to come through solid substances, as walls, etc., to be re-formed into its original physical state in the presence of the medium. Thus the theory is strengthened that the guides are masters in the art of controlling energies.

Hence we can begin to understand one of the methods by which harmful substances within our bodies can be quickly removed. The taking away of a substance must be either carried out in this fashion or its formation so altered that it can be dispersed through the bloodstream or evacuated from the body in some other way.

We have to give the healing guides the credit of differentiating between harmful cells or substances and healthy ones. With the removal of a cataract it is only the obstructing film that is dispersed, leaving the eye uninjured.

* See *The Mediumship of Jack Webber* by Harry Edwards.

However far-fetched this theory may appear, we have to account for the fact that substances can be dispersed in a fragment of time. It is therefore logical to conclude that a state of change has been induced in the condition of the offending matter. When a substance has been proved to exist, and then with healing found to have disappeared, we must earnestly consider the process of de-materialising as feasible.

After all, when doctors apply deep-ray therapy they are only following a similar process. The doctors direct a dispersing energy or force that breaks up and destroys diseased cells.

If we agree that to the guides the manipulation of energies is a much more simple matter than it is to Harwell, we can more readily appreciate the way of healing by the means of applying a disrupting force to break up the atomic formation of a cancer cell.

It must not be assumed however that all healings are instantaneous. Indeed, the majority of healings take time, which indicates that the application of the remedial forces employed need to be continuously applied to overcome progressively the trouble.

Different qualities of healing force are needed to deal with each given condition. There are the diseases that need the "nourishment energy" to build up and restore the good health of the cells. Doctors attempt to rectify this by introducing the lacking quality through medicine, injections and other means. If the cells are lacking in a particular element, the guides, aware of the deficiency, direct the missing force that is the replica of the energies that go to make up the atomic element to the cells, which when transformed into a physical state supply the missing quality.

Stimulating forces are also employed. This is observed with conditions of wastage, with depreciated tissues as seen with polio-myelitis, atrophies and nerve weaknesses and with forms of paralysis. As the healing effort is sustained so the tissues become more healthy, muscular formations are restored and the nerves are revitalised to enable easier co-ordination. While these results may, in part, be a reaction from the impetus directed to the body intelligence, experience shows that a form of stimulation or new energy is imparted to strengthen the weakened state.

Most patients receiving spiritual healing become aware in the early days of a feeling of upliftment and well-being. While this may result from mental easement, and it is impossible to separate this from organic healing, the new sensing gives a happier condition to the body. There is lightness in action, freedom from fatigue, indicating that a general tonic or vitalising force has been applied. This is invariably seen, as the first stage in the healing of anæmia and blood diseases. Thus it may well be that there is a type of healing force that acts as a general stimulant.

To attain a clearer acceptance of the application and character of the healing forces, it is necessary to keep in mind that every atom of which we are composed is a perfectly organised energy machine governed by laws that not only maintain its individuality but enable it to blend with other atoms where receptivity exists between them. Study of atomic structures will illustrate this fact. As one form of energy is associated with another so a different result will arise. Healings therefore come from a corrective application of remedial, characterised energy to the ill-condition, thereby inducing a beneficial change.

So far, only energies applicable to the healing of organic conditions have been mentioned. Those connected with mental healing are dealt with in a later chapter.

The ability of the guides to change the consistency of diseased matter is illustrated by the two following instances.

A man had a tumour in the throat. His condition was very obvious. He could not speak or swallow food, and had to be fed through a tube. The doctors considered the condition to be too severe to operate and decided that nothing more could be done for him except nursing. The wife telephoned for healing, and during the night that followed the man vomited masses of *loose* matter. It is important to note that the substance of this matter was very loose and not at all consistent with the fleshy structure of the tumour. When the vomiting was over, it was clear that the tumour had gone. The man was able to talk and before long could swallow food normally once again.

The second case refers to a woman who had an abdominal cancer of an advanced order. Her body had been opened up and the cancer seen to be inoperable. The growth had infiltrated throughout the body. The body was sewn up and she was sent home to end her days. The only treatment given to her was the administration of morphia to lessen her pains. During the twenty-four hours after I had been taken to see her she passed through the rectum excessive motions of a queer nature. In a day or so she was up and about, engaged on her household duties and lived for some years afterwards.

In both these cases a change had been effected in the nature of the substance of the growths—they had been rendered into a semifluid condition. In the second case, while this was not provable, the implication is that the change in the status and the expulsion of the cancer applied to the infiltrations as well as to the central mass of the growth. Thus we have evidence that the healing forces can not only disperse directly, by breaking up the atomic formation of the elements, but in other cases, where the trouble can be evacuated from the body, induce a change in the structure of all the harmful matter, permitting its expulsion. It is interesting to observe how correct must be the guides' diagnosis and understanding of the need to be able to decide upon which method is most beneficial for the patient.

When healers are giving contact healing they are often aware of the sensation of strong heat or cold when the hand is in close proximity to the ill-condition. As the hand moves away so the sensation diminishes. The patient can feel the heat or the cold as a deeply penetrating force. This heat is not clinical. If a thermometer is interposed between the healer's hand and the patient it does not register any change of temperature. While we do not know of any particular service those heat or cold sensations give, we know that they are forces created in the healing act. Suffice it that these sensations cannot be induced at will but only in the healing act. They cannot be the result of increased circulation within the healer's hand for obvious reasons. These heat and cold forces usually come when dealing with such troubles as rheumatism, fibrositis and arthritis, and are experienced generally whenever there is an organic ill-condition. That they are remedial healing forces is beyond question—as every healer knows. Following this experience a reduction of the trouble is most often seen.

CHAPTER TEN

WHY SOME HEALINGS FAIL

One day, a mother brought her few months old baby to me. The little one was perfect in every way except that the feet were noticeably contorted with an inward turn. The balls of the feet and the toes were stretched downwards. The doctors had told the mother that it would be advisable to postpone any surgical or manipulative treatment until the child was a little older. The point of this story is that to me both feet were affected in an identical manner. I took one foot in my hands, sought for healing aid, and ever so gently moved the foot up and round. Within my hand I could feel the changing in position taking place. When I took my hands away the foot was facing forwards and could move up and down in a normal manner. So next came the other foot, but with this I was unable to discern any change at all. It remained contorted and restricted in movement. This greatly intrigued me. I saw the baby on two further occasions, without obtaining any response. It was on the fourth visit, when the baby was nearly one year old, that the foot responded and the child could begin to stand squarely on both feet. The problem in this case was: Why, with seemingly two identical conditions with the same baby, had one foot yielded immediately to the healing, and the other did not respond until some six months afterwards in spite of repeated efforts being made?

The second case concerns the passing of my friend, Jack Webber, who in the 1940's was one of our outstanding physical mediums. We had been daily companions for over two years. There had not been one ill-thought between us as I sponsored his mediumship and looked after his interests. Suddenly he became ill. I knew intuitively the illness was very serious. I felt so acutely for him that I was willing to draw the trouble from him into myself. Now I know that I should not have sought to do this, nor could it have been possible, but I mention the fact to indicate the depth of affection that I had for him. He passed into spirit life some three days later, when it was pathologically established that Jack had contracted a virulent form of spinal meningitis. It is noteworthy to recall that at no time did he suffer any bodily stress. Usually with this disease the days previous to a passing in normal cases are most distressful and agonising ones. My last memory of him was on the evening before his release from earth life. I was sitting on his bed and together we were singing his favourite song, "Danny Boy". During the night he lost consciousness. His body stiffened and he was taken to hospital, where the final change shortly took place. The importance of this story is in the sequel.

The following week brought into my shop a mother and father who had specially broken their journey from the North of England to Portsmouth to see if I could obtain spirit healing for their son who was dying from spinal meningitis. They had been urgently asked to go down to Portsmouth in view of the seriousness of their son's condition. Indeed they expected to find him dead by the time they reached the hospital and so had made the break in their journey as a last hope.

With the recent memory of Jack and spinal meningitis in my mind, I felt very sorry for the parents. I went into the quiet and sought help for the lad. When the parents arrived at the hospital and entered their son's ward, they were astonished to find him sitting up in bed, with four doctors in conference around him, studying what, to them, was nothing more than a "miracle." All trace of the disease had left him. The doctors "wondered where he had got his strength from," and in a few days he was home. It transpired that the patient was a soldier belonging to the Hussar Regiment. So complete was his recovery that he was able to return to full duty. This fact makes the healing all the more remarkable when it is remembered the complications that so often follow in the train of this disease.

Thus I was faced with a problem that did little to ease my mind of the sadness at the passing of Jack and actually made me feel a little bitter about things. Why was it that my dearest friend, with his close attunement to his own spirit guides, and who had so often been the means of healing the sick, plus the help from my healing guides from whom I so dearly sought help, should not have been helped to recover, while a perfect stranger, one I had never seen before and since, should be helped so much? It was very hard to understand.

From these experiences I learned the lesson that no one case can be taken as a precedent for another, not even with one foot as to the other.

With this conclusion, we have a position that may create some difficulty in obtaining medical co-operation, for doctors are accustomed to expecting predetermined results from definite treatments. They rely on their knowledge of anatomy and the chemistry of the body, so that when they administer a specific medicine they should see the anticipated change take place. With spiritual healing this is not so. We cannot give any promise or undertaking in advance for any person that a healing result will occur. We cannot call for healing "on demand," even though we can visualise the postulates that bring it into being.

In our analyses of healing results there appears to be approximately twenty per cent. who do not record improvement. As a rule all those who request spiritual healing do so because they have lost their faith in doctors or are afraid of what the medical diagnosis and treatment may be, or in the great majority of cases because the trouble does not yield to medical treatment, or the doctors have said they are "incurable". Considering these factors twenty per cent. lack of beneficial result is a very favourable figure, yet we must be concerned with it. Just as there must be a reasoned process behind every healing, so there must also exist reasons why no response is apparently seen—all other contingencies being equal.

It has already been shown that the limit that governs healing is the total laws that control our well-being from conception (and even before conception) to passing. One of these limitations is that, in time, the energies comprising the atomic structures begin to lose their force, as is seen with stone and oak. With all animal life this limitation is very much more marked, and deterioration in function as age advances is just one of the penalties of being born. Perhaps it is not a penalty, for it is doubtful if one would wish to live for ever. In the greater scheme of things it would prevent our enjoyment of the spiritual heritage that we enter after this phase of life has ended. Just as the metamorphosis of the caterpillar into a chrysalis state and thence into the final butterfly stage to carry on the species is a law of life, so our metamorphosis is likewise the law. Thus it may often be that when healing does not appear to take place it can well be for the reason that the time has come for the change to take place.

It is also the law that "effects follow causes." Should it be that the physical cause of a complaint is persisted in then a healing cannot be fulfilled. To prove this point, the examples of waning eye sight and arthritis have been mentioned earlier in this book. To recapitulate: if a person's sight is weakening through eye strain induced by close work in daily employment, and this is persisted in, then the return of the full sight is prevented, although the healing will maintain it in as good a condition as the circumstances allow. If a patient suffering from rheumatism, arthritis or fibrositis has to work outside in inclement weather or sleeps in a damp bed, the healing effort must be largely negative. Thus in a number of cases the full healing depends upon obeying the laws of health.

I recall one patient who was suffering badly from arthritis. I noted that she had a number of badly decayed teeth. It seemed probable that the teeth were promoting toxic conditions that interfered with the health of the bloodstream. I ventured to suggest that she had all these bad teeth out, which she would not do, because she had a fear of dental treatment. Her arthritis was eased but did not clear, and she would have been registered as a "failure". Eventually she plucked up courage and had her mouth attended to and dentures supplied. From this date her arthritis progressively disappeared until she was free of the trouble.

When the cause of the disease has its origin in mental and inner-self disharmony, the progress of the healing will depend upon the rapidity with which corrective influencing from Spirit is able to soothe and calm the upsets. With some people the inner frustration has become so deep-seated that it has become woven into the pattern of life. It may be with such people the progress of the healing is far from what we would wish to see.

Many times, the help of spirit healing is enlisted during the critical days before a passing. The doctors have said that the person is unlikely to live more than a few days. The distressed relatives in a last act of desperation come to the healer. While occasionally recoveries from such chronic states do take place they are not the general rule. The healing is said to have failed. In this respect, when a recovery is not within the scheme of things, there is no question that help from Spirit is given. Instead of a troubled and painful passing, the patient loses the sense of pain. Comfort, inner-strength and peacefulness come to the mind. The patient sleeps without the need for drugs and the passing is free from stress. While such a case is listed as a failure, it is questionable whether it really comes within that category.

In this connection I would like to tell of my mother's health history. Some years ago she was sadly troubled with attacks of giddiness and heart weaknesses. Her doctor expressed the opinion that she might pass away at any time from a heart attack. Naturally we sought healing aid for her, and not only did the giddy attacks completely vanish but so did all symptoms of heart strain. My mother, in her ninety-second year, is in full possession of all her functions except hearing. She is robust and in reasonably good health. As her hearing waned so came the distress of head noises. I tried to seek their removal but without result. Then one day, my mother asked Olive Burton, who with her husband have been my very dear and close collaborators for the past twelve years, to attempt to take away the noises. This Mrs. Burton did. From that moment the noises ceased and for some years she has not been troubled in this way. Yet the deafness continues, and in spite of all our seeking it does not diminish. The reason probably is that with her advanced age the faculty of hearing has deteriorated into a senile state. It may be said that the healing has failed to restore her hearing and she should be registered as a "failure," but in view of the many other ways she has been healed this would surely be a wrong description.

There is another factor to consider in the discussion of "failures". It has been previously pointed out that every healing must result from an intelligent administration of corrective healing forces within the law. By "intelligent administration" is meant the extent of the wisdom of the spirit guides to produce a satisfactory change. We should be in error if we ascribed to the intelligences who are the healing guides all wisdom and omnipotent power. They, too, have need to acquire knowledge, through experience. This takes place progressively as they study more closely our needs and the potentials within the healing forces. Evidence of this has been seen with the healing of certain troubles, as with poker-back spines. To-day, this condition yields far more easily and quickly than it did, say, ten years ago, establishing the evidence that the guides have advanced in their knowledge and ability to cope with this particular trouble. A similar story can be related to the dispersal of cataracts and growths, etc. Thus spirit healing is ever progressing. Conditions that do not appear to respond readily to-day may do so in the future.

In the endeavour to assess the reasons for non-success, there are other factors to be taken into consideration besides those already mentioned.

One of these is that the patient has become so used to the adverse effects produced by the disease that the perpetuation of the symptoms has become a fixed habit of the body. If we assume that a hip or knee joint has suffered for a number of years from pain or locking, the patient has got into the firm habit of walking with the leg stiff, and possibly swinging it from the pelvis. With the healing, the disability is removed, and under the healer's direction the patient is able to circulate the joints freely and normally without any pain at all. He is shown that he can now walk properly, but even with this object lesson it will at times be seen that as a matter of habit he returns to the former method of walking with the leg stiff. So it is said he is no better for the healing. If the cause of the immobility is arthritis and no advantage is taken to sustain the restored loose movement, then it is likely that the joint will stiffen once again.

Fear is another cause of patients refusing to acknowledge the healing result. They are afraid that if they continue to take advantage of the healing benefit the pains will return. They take refuge in returning to the limiting conditions to which they have become accustomed as being painless.

Then the healer has to meet those whose mind is firmly fixed on their infirmity; it has become part of their way of living. The words, "I cannot do that" has become so deep-rooted that they will not on any account use their bodies more freely, even though the healing has removed the weakness and stress.

There is also that class of people who would not be happy unless they have the infirmity perpetuated, so that they can receive sympathy from others. Even though they seek the good that spirit healing can do for them they do not really want to respond.

Healers also have to deal with hypochondriacs who maintain a list of imaginary complaints. With these healing is said to fail because the patients persist in believing themselves to be ill when they are not.

When all these factors are considered it will be seen that the twenty per cent. for whom a good report cannot be given would be greatly reduced.

The healer has to learn that he should not blame himself or his healing gift for any lack of success. There is a good reason for it. Neither should he blame the patient, and definitely not the healing guide.

Now that man understands a little of the nature of energies locked in the atom, spiritual healing comes within the rational field. It can be explained in terms of laws parallel to those which rule healing success and also non-success. The power to repair wasted tissue, to restore nervous force, to cleanse the physical body from disease, to repair broken minds, to bring new light to darkened intelligence, is the result of applied power in a planned way.

Only because we are more scientific in our approach to these matters can we become more spiritual. That is to say: only as we increase our real knowledge of the forces of nature and the spirit can we align our moralities and lives to come within the borders of these truths. Only because we have come slowly upwards from a pit of deep ignorance dug by priests and others throughout the ages can we understand now that the healing miracles of Jesus were manifestations of the same knowledge to use the power as we are witnessing to-day. That mankind did not learn from Christ's teachings is not the fault of God who sent Him or of His disciples. They did all that they could. Nearly two thousand years have had to elapse before we have been able to learn sufficient to appreciate the nature of matter and the existence and co-operation of Spirit.

It may seem a long way from the understanding of both success and non-success in the healing of a broken body to the secrets within the atomic energies, but all is interwoven for good in the end. Without our modern knowledge of radio, radar and atomic energy it would be harder to explain the wonder and existence of the soul and spirit healing. Perhaps that is why true religion has languished for so long; there was not enough knowledge to make spirit healing credible. The Church in the past, as well as ignorant men greedy for power, created dictatorships for the enslavement of the uninformed. The only outpourings of the Spirit were in the realms of the arts and in the slow and painful march of reform and tolerance.

Now that we have more knowledge to comprehend the capabilities and limitations of healing, the work of the Spirit can go ahead. In the healing effort, even though unsuccessful, good work is done. In healing there is ordered progress. It works from good to better and thence to greater good, until, one day, in some far distant time, man will truly heal himself since he will fully know himself and his spirit-self.

CHAPTER ELEVEN

MENTAL HEALING

It is in the field of mental healing that spiritual healing excels. It is quite a different character of activity to the healing of organic conditions employing the use of energies relating to matter.

The nearest approach we can make to this in life is telepathy, which today is accepted as proven by many scientists. There can be no doubt that our consciousness is receptive to influencing by thought from Spirit. Apart from healing, clairvoyance clearly indicates that minds attuned to receptivity of thought direction from Spirit can receive detailed mental pictures and messages.

It is a truism that no disease or ill-condition can be cured until the cause is overcome. Spirit healing removes the cause and then assists in removing the symptoms. This explains why through spirit healing we so often see those thought by doctors to be incurable get well. The reader is again asked to bear in mind that all authorities now agree that the greater percentage of physical ailments have their primary causation in some form of mind or inner-self unrest. The percentage has been judged by some authorities as high as eighty. Some healers think that it may well be higher, for diseases such as cancer (which the medical profession is not yet willing to admit is caused in this way) may well come under the general conclusion.

When the cause of disease originates within the total mind, medicine can do little or nothing to overcome it and is perforce restricted to palliative drugs and measures for treating only the symptoms. Thus it is that when the cause of a so-called incurable condition lies in mental and spirit-mind disharmony—and this can be calmed and soothed by corrective influencing from Spirit—it is mastered and the "incurable" physical effects yield to the healing. It is upon this conclusion that much of our understanding of the means and processes employed by the spirit healing intelligences rests.

It is necessary to consider the human mind as being in two sections: the physical mind that is concerned with earthly experiences, the garnering of knowledge, the comfort of the body and the smooth working of its systems. Then there is the spirit mind that is building character, the seat of the conscience, and which has as its concern ambition, expression of purposes, and the primal qualities that animate our being, love and hatred, kindness and cruelty, generosity and meanness, sacrifice and selfishness, etc.

The two minds are intimately akin to each other; one can influence the other. Characters can be ennobled or demeaned. If the physical mind is centred on the seeking of power or lustful satisfactions, it is the finer spirit self that can change these directives. On the other hand when, in physical life, we are swayed by the written or spoken word to enagage in good services so can the spirit self be strengthened.

Consider the philosophy of the Germans in the last war. Many were inculcated with hatred towards the Jews, they were imbued with those brutal doctrines with which our memories are still familiar. As these became dominant directives so it followed that the spiritual motives of their lives became dulled and decadent. This is a simple illustration of how the physical approach to life can influence one's spiritual progress for good or ill. It is noteworthy that to-day the mass German opinion repudiates the wartime Teutonic atrocities.

Conversely, the right influencing from the spirit self can induce good changes in the way of life. It is our common experience to see these spiritual changes take place. Here is a typical story. A wife wrote very distressingly that her husband had, for no reason known to her, changed into a different man. He had become sadistic and cruel, vicious in temperament towards her and their children, so much so that they feared his coming into the house. She asked for help for her husband and for strength and guidance for herself. A few days after she received my first letter it was happily apparent that her husband's nature was changing for the better. Before long he had regained his kindness and love for his family. In the letters that followed it was disclosed that the husband was aware of his relapse and did all that he could to recompense his dear ones. After some time the wife thought she would tell her husband how it was that the good change had come. She was apprehensive in doing so, for she knew her husband had little time for "religion." When she did pluck up courage enough to tell him, his reply was simple; it was just two words, "Thank God."

How these good changes come about is illustrated by another story. This also tells of domestic misery, somewhat similar to the previous story but with the additional factor that the man was addicted to drink, on which he spent much of his earnings and providing very little for the home. By absent healing, we sought for good influences to reach him. One day as the man was returning home, he felt an irresistible impulse to go into a shop and buy some flowers. He said afterwards he felt rather "a ninny" in carrying the flowers home, yet he had an inner joy in doing so. When he arrived he thrust the flowers into his wife's hands without saying a word. She was dumbfounded as she asked, "What are these for?" His abrupt reply was, "For you." That was the beginning of a return of love and happiness into the home, and the drink habit passed away.

In studying this true story, one asks whence came the impulse to influence the man to buy the flowers? It was foreign to his mind. It was a thought that normally he would have scornfully rejected, yet he was impelled to carry it out. We suggest that just when the moment was favourable the guides directed him, through his spirit mind, to stimulate his conscious action.

In similar fashion alcoholics and drug addicts respond to this treatment. A doctor who conducted a nursing home for drug addicts in Bournemouth would seek through absent healing for difficult patients to be helped to master their weaknesses. The beneficial results were such that the doctor could date the change for the better with the start of the healing effort.

Thus the healing for mental disharmonies is often direct in restoring balance, but, perhaps, more often it is indirect, for the patients are not aware of the gravity of their shortcomings.

One of the easiest healings of this kind is seen with those mothers who, after childbirth, lose their sense of proportion. They become frantic and often will not tolerate the presence of their husbands, nor do they want to see their baby. At times this upset becomes so strong that they have to be admitted into a mental hospital for treatment. Obviously the cause is temporary and not inherent. In every case of this nature when healing intervention has been sought there has been a rapid return to normality.

The calming and soothing of mind frustrations has been observed in a very great number of cases of divergent characteristics. There is that class of patient who has a persecution-complex. Others torture themselves with suspicions that their partner is unfaithful to them. There are those who have a complex that everything they come into contact with is dirty and are continually washing themselves. Then there are those who have no faith in their checking or counting and need to re-check again and again.

We have to deal with that further class of people who are obsessed and hear "voices," and still another whose daily outlook is tortured by remorse over some past experience. Then there are the many sections of mental sickness that arise from claustrophobia, the fear of going out, of meeting people, against types of food, shyness, blushing and so on.

Doctors can do very little for these people; neither can the well-intentioned preaching of parsons. Some receive the full measure of prescribed medical electric shock treatment, insulin, induced sleep and so on, unfortunately with little remedial effect in most cases. As a rule the minds of the sick need calming and soothing and should not be further disturbed by electric shocks. Above all, each needs individual understanding. Though credit must be given to doctors who seek this, they are limited in their therapies and so most of these patients are subjected to the shock, insulin and sleep treatments. In some cases normality follows the natural return of perspective and contentment of outlook. These comprise the bulk of healings attributed to medical practice.

With all forms of mental sickness it is abundantly clear that each patient has an individual trouble needing the particular understanding of its cause. This understanding of the inner mind is, mainly, outside the scope of another human mind to appreciate. Psychiatry endeavours to seek out the causes by interrogation, and often only brings the fears, etc., into prominence again. Even when the psychiatrist is able to find the cause, he is unable to prescribe any form of treatment or to give any counsel that is of any avail.

The healing of the mind must take place on the same level as it exists. As almost all these troubles have their origin within the spirit mind they can be helped only from the spirit level. This provides the reason why mental disharmonies yield readily to spiritual healing. When the origin is contained more within the physical mind, the healing influences are able to reach this through the spirit mind which is in such close affinity to the other.

Just as the patient is able to describe his fears and symptoms, so it is reasonable to assume that the spirit guides are able to see these clearly within his mind, which is an "open book" to them. Therefore the guides are able to direct those correcting thoughts and directives to unravel the upset condition and restore perspective.

Another way in which healing has proved beneficial is the awakening of co-ordination of the minds of backward children, to kindle the responsibilities of the conscience, and bring an awareness of right and wrong. These unformed minds need to be led gently into the way of appreciating life, and to induce creative thought. While the healing directive can do a great deal, much depends upon the help and encouragement that the parents and others can patiently give.

With more serious complications, where a sense such as sight is missing, here again the assistance healing gives to enable the consciousness to become receptive to impression cannot be underrated. As a rule these healings are not rapid, as can be well appreciated, but with continued and constant application of the healing purpose many unfortunate young people have been helped to a greater or lesser extent. It should, however, be said that when the very nature of a child has been ill-formed from biological reasons from previous generations, such as with mongol and cretin children, we do not see the nature of the child transformed. At the same time many children who are said to be spastic, resulting from palsy, often respond well through the combination of mental and physical healing.

Measurable good is also seen in accelerating the return of co-ordination and control with the effects of paralysis that follow strokes, etc. In these cases the healing purpose is directed to the mind, to soothe the shock and upset to the motor nerves and allow the messages from the mind to travel through the nerve cells so as to restore co-ordinated movement once again. This healing too is gradual, but there is plenty of evidence to show how much more rapidly a recovery takes place with the intervention of the healing directive.

The healing of epilepsy presents a more complicated problem; much depends upon the character of the sickness. If it is inherited from the parents a full healing does not often take place, but the severity and number of attacks is diminished. It may be that many people who suffer from attacks that are similar in effect to epilepsy are not affected by this disease at all, but from lack of maintained mental control within the consciousness. When the trouble is of this nature and is not inherent, but the result of some dire experience or shock, the gradual progressive healing is often seen as the attacks lose their power and the time between them extends more and more until normality is regained.

When I commenced my healing ministry I was called upon to deal with a number of cases of skin disease which responded wonderfully well. At that time I was strongly of the impression that most skin troubles arise from nervous tensions, temperaments and frustrations; subsequent study of the background behind the patients proved this contention to the hilt. It was therefore with some justifiable pleasure that I read some years later how the medical profession had made a great discovery, that the cause of some skin diseases arose from mental causes.

Three cases come to mind. The first was of a young woman suffering from a severe condition of psoriasis. She was very distressed because when she undressed the scales of skin would fall from her like confetti, and she was to be married in a few weeks time. With the commencement of the healing she said how she felt that a weight had been lifted from her mind. She began to experience the sensing of supreme happiness and with this the skin trouble quickly vanished.

The second case, I shall give in the words of the doctor in charge of the case: "Three years ago the patient contracted a skin disease known as *Sycocis Barbae,* an intractable and very distressing complaint. For reasons connected with the war, it was the better part of a year before he could obtain expert treatment (he was a prisoner of war). The specialists then informed him that, owing to the delay, the prospects of a cure were very remote. I mentioned the case to a colleague who replied, 'Having no treatment for nine months, he will be fortunate if he is cured in nine years.' For nearly two years he attended the skin departments of various hospitals in London and in the provinces. Although a temporary improvement was occasionally observed, the sores on his face did not heal and the area they covered slowly increased. Last April I asked Edwards to treat the case. When I saw the patient about a fortnight ago his face had entirely healed, nothing remaining but the pale scars where the sores had been. As in other cases that I have seen treated by Edwards the cure was at first gradual, then suddenly the healing process accelerated until the sores disappeared."

The third case was that of a young boy, about nine years old, whose body was covered with skin eruptions. The parents said that owing to his crying they had not had even one night's sleep since he was born. I went to see this boy, who was of an excitable temperament, rarely still, and would not concentrate on anything for long. I placed my hands on his head and sought for peace to come to his mind. For the whole of that night he slept peacefully.

His temperament showed a change gradually becoming more orderly. In a very short time the skin cleared and he became more contented and happy.

These illustrations clearly indicate that the healing purpose must first overcome the cause of the trouble by corrective influencing to the mind, cleansing it of frustrative tendencies.

There are occasions when, to outward appearances, patients suffering from a physical disease, that is the general outcome of mind tensions, are calm and contented in their outlook. In these cases, it may be that the cause of unrest is subconscious, or may exist in a suppressed desire for expression within the spirit self to be fulfilled. An instance could be an inner desire to engage in some art or pursuit that normal life does not permit. There may have been some experience in early life that has registered a permanent state of unrest or fear.

I remember when I was very young my father telling me about one of his boyhood experiences when a fish bone caught in his throat and he nearly suffocated before it was extracted. As a result, all through my life I have been exceedingly careful about fish bones, and feel at times a little apprehensive for others who are eating fish in my presence. Thus, this seemingly unimportant incident made an indelible impression on my consciousness that revives a condition of fear when there is cause for it.

We also know that a terrifying experience that happened in the life of an ancestor can have its presence inducted into the personality of the living person to-day. This does not necessarily support the theory of reincarnation but is a biological carry-on from the genes in the life cells of the parent.

Such tendencies are obviously beyond the influence of the doctor, and can only be soothed by inculcating a sense of perspective within the spirit-self of the patient.

A final example of how mental tension can produce physical ill-effects is supplied by the admitted general cause of gastric ulcers, pains and abdominal upsets through worry, anxieties and responsibilities. Figures prove that professions which carry much mental responsibility are far more addicted to abdominal troubles than other ways of life where this factor is not so acutely present.

With these gastric and other troubles, the healing can generally remove the symptoms easily by soothing the present tensions, though it may take longer to eliminate the cause. This aspect of healing introduces consideration of the value of psychology in healing. The right psychological approach to a patient is of great importance. The appeal to his common sense to appreciate the cause of his trouble. Advising him not to bring home his business worries. Suggesting that he seeks enjoyment of life's purpose and has some recreation. All these can often assist the healing effort to promote tranquillity in the outlook.

In healing it is important to maintain an expectantly hopeful attitude of mind, looking for easement to come. We take issue with many doctors who are prone to tell their patients of all the possible adverse complications that may arise. As I write these words I have a wife's letter to answer. Her husband, suffering from an internal complaint, has been making satisfactory progress with our healing. His outlook has been happy. The symptoms of stress were effectively diminishing, when he saw his doctor who bluntly told him there was no medical cure. The doctor foretold the progressive worsening of his condition until he would become bedfast, helpless and have increasing pain as the disease developed, and that he would have to learn to live with it until he died. This unnecessary and cruel description plunged the man into the depths of black despair. He could not free his mind from the burden he would become to his dear ones. Unfortunately, this is not an isolated instance; we have had many other similar stories narrated to us where doctors dismally prophesy woeful futures. The purpose of healing, and this includes medical treatments, should be to sustain morale and not destroy it. Most medical men recognise the tremendous advantage in maintaining a good psychological approach with their patients, amply illustrated in the preparation of patients for surgery.

It is admitted that one of the most serious factors in surgery is the shock administered to the patient during the operation and in its anticipation. It has been seen over and over again that when inner strength and assurance through spiritual healing have been directed for a patient before undergoing a major operation he receives a response in a vitality that sustains him through the operation speedily and well, provides a good outlook and confidence and an absence of fear. When we assure a patient that help and strength from Spirit will be with them, and this is accepted by the mind, aided by the good calming and reassuring thoughts from Spirit, apprehensions and fears are overcome. The mind is led to co-operate with the surgery. The element of shock is greatly reduced and the surgeons comment on the excellent way the patients have come through the ordeal with unexpected calm and strength; so much so, that they are able to leave the hospital days before the normal time needed for recovery.

It is apparent that when the inner-mind is unhappy it affects the whole physical condition. It is as a cloud of depression that darkens the daily life. It weakens vitality, the health tone suffers, and the physical body becomes more vulnerable to diseases, infections, influenzas and other troubles. The good that spirit healing does in maintaining a good health tone must not be underestimated, as has already been mentioned; one of the first signs with the healing of many diseases is that the patient experiences a sense of inner-upliftment in the early stages.

It is important for the healer to show how fears and tensions can be dissipated. This is not difficult. It is useless just to tell the patient "not to worry," or to concentrate on religion or, indeed, anything else, for this only introduces another worrying factor. It is our general practice to encourage the return of peacefulness, assurance and confidence in a natural and simple way by asking the patient to look for happiness in all the small things of life. We ask him to be happy when the kettle boils, to take an interest on the way to work in the neighbours' front gardens, to greet all the people he meets with a smile, to have a smile for himself. We ask him to take pride in his appearance. If the patient is a woman we suggest that she puts on her brightest clothes and listens to "Housewife's Choice" on the wireless, to make herself up a little, present a good appearance, to have pride in herself and to make an appetising supper for her husband. We often tell a man to take his wife or children some sweets and to enter more fully into the happiness of home affairs. As patients do this they cannot help but co-operate with the encouraging and good influences being directed from Spirit through their inner-minds, to create that more carefree and contented outlook.

True, this is perhaps just good psychology, but healing is not only psychology but psychology plus healing.

It is a solemn yet satisfying thought that there are these unseen spirit personalities who send the healing thoughts to those in need, resulting in peaceful sleep and forgetfulness of fears by absolving mental tortures. To so many can come this healing balm, this restorer of happiness in life's purpose, this nourisher of the human frame. To a large number this first contact with healing is the beginning of a new lease of life. Some who formerly walked bent, not with physical disease but through distortion of the mind, stand erect once more and look wonderful to those who love them. Others, after years of misery, feel full of energy and find that life has again become good to live. They are of all kinds, for the total laws under which we freely live are no respecters of persons, be he one who is suffering in the terrible darkness of religious mania, the woman whose home has become a prison, the wife who sees her husband kindly and attentive again, and the one who has recovered his self-confidence and assurance.

I could write of the girl with convulsive attacks of a dangerous kind who was placed in a padded cell to prevent self-inflicted injuries and was cured; the father who had suicidal tendencies; the mother who had the urge to hurt her children; the girl who could not sleep and spent the long hours of the night in a chair or walking about; the man who kept checking his figures over and over again; the girl who washed her hands scores of times each day; the many who were afraid to go out and locked themselves in rooms away from their families. All of them have been restored to happy living. But there is no room, neither is there space for all the gratitude we should express to the healing guides.

Long after we who are so privileged to take part in this work have passed from the earthly scene there will be arguments to determine how it all began and how it took place. But, as I see it, we all do all that we can. Even the sufferer who is certified insane and is later cured by the silent invisible forces is part of the drama of the restoration to mankind of truths which should never have been forsaken. The drama will continue to unfold in the days to come, to provide a happier heritage for our children than we have known. The truth and value of what are here recorded will remain.

It is a dark though wonderful world from which we are emerging. Alas there are still many who obscure the light from the vision of those who should have it by right of birth into the human family. The great comforting, healing and teaching mission, which is the heart and centre of Spiritualism, would not have been necessary had man followed the charted path. But it was not so, and many efforts have been made throughout time to help the victims of false teachings and ignorance. Spiritual healing is one aspect of the regenerative work. As it succeeds the burden of the human race will be lightened. This is the motive behind spiritual healing leading to the spiritualisation of mankind. Because it is true, it will endure.

CHAPTER TWELVE

"FAITH" HEALING

The term "faith healing" is often applied to spiritual healing, without reason or understanding, through common usuage, mainly sustained by the Press.

Faith healing implies the strong belief of a patient to get well. It may be founded on the religious belief that "with God all things are possible," or on the claim associated with Christian Science that creation is perfect and therefore imperfections exist only in the mind. It can be based on the personal exercise of will power that there can be no surrender to physical weaknesses and that through strong, purposeful thought application an ill-condition can be overcome.

It is closely allied with the psychological approach to disease by Coueism, in which the positive thought directive is that "every day and in every way I am getting better and better."

Faith healing is obviously the product of the self. While this can often assist in mastering a complaint it is widely divorced from spiritual healing.

Other terms have been applied to spiritual healing. The Church calls it divine healing. Some psychics call it psychic healing. Lately there have come into being all sorts of pseudo-scientific terms like parapsychosis. I suggest that by whatever name spirit healing is called, it is the same thing, even if it be termed by the misnomer of "faith healing." It is obvious that there is not one set of healing processes specially created for the Church in divine healing and another set for the Spiritualist in spiritual healing. The field of healing belongs to the one means, although there are different methods of approaching it and benefiting from it.

Spiritual healing is a spirit science. As has been pointed out, it is an individually planned act needing intelligent administration by minds that are much further advanced in knowledge than are human ones.

The proof that spiritual healing is not faith healing is simply established by the fact that babies and little children are healed of disease when, of course, they are too young to possess any faith. Again many people who respond are very weak and in pain. They are unable to have that sure faith that they will get well. Then there is the class of patient for whom absent healing is sought by a third party. This, a common occurrence, arises from the good intention of the third party to seek help for people, such as Roman Catholics and atheists, who would not be willing or agreeable to receive aid from this source. There is yet another section, those suffering from a so-called "incurable" disease of which they are ignorant. That these people are healed just as those who are knowledgeable of the act is beyond dispute.

In general, absent healing proves this too. The healer is not in personal contact with the patients, many of whom have no knowledge of the source whence comes the benefits they are receiving.

If faith alone could heal the sick, we should see the hospitals quickly emptied. But all the faith in the world cannot change the blood content of a blue baby or unlock the cemented joint of an arthritic condition.

Faith is not reason, it is just belief. I have met those good people who possess such abounding faith that they will not even consider the possibility of a dear one who is gravely ill failing to get well. Unfortunately if a passing takes place it creates a mental shock that does great harm, bringing depression and despair, for they receive a very deep mental wound. Mostly we see this attitude of mind with Church people. It is doubtless encouraged by the teaching that if they have "faith enough" God will answer their prayers. So these people build up within their minds absolute faith that their dear ones will be made well. Indeed, a common excuse used by priests, when prayers have been said for a sick one without avail and a passing ensues, is that the relatives "did not have enough faith" for God to act. This disregards the point of view that the clergymen himself should possess that abounding faith as an ordained priest of God.

Faith in healing is of course most helpful—in the same way that a patient has belief in his doctor and the bottle of medicine to do him good. It is a psychological asset.

When appointments are made for patients to come to the Sanctuary we enclose instructions. In these we prepare them not to expect a miracle or a rapid cure, but that we will seek healing aid to reach them to the extent that becomes possible. I recall a tragic case of a young woman who, as a child, had had poliomyelitis. As a result her legs were quite useless. They had not even grown and no reaction of movement could be induced in them by her. With relatives, she had come to the Sanctuary on the offchance that we would see her. We sought help for her in every possible way, but we did not succeed in getting any movement in the legs. No doubt the nerves had completely gone. When we had finished, she asked if she could send a telegram to her mother who was waiting to hear that she could walk. Such blind faith is distressing. It may not be the patients' fault but that of over-enthusiastic people who have told them: "You only have to see Harry Edwards and for him to touch you to be healed." Even with Jesus it was not everyone who was made well. Even He could not act contrary to the laws of creation. We can truly appreciate this in the New Testament words, "And many were healed," and not "all were healed."

Occasionally we read in a letter of the despair that Church-inspired "blind faith" has brought. We are asked: "Why has God taken our dear one away—he was so good and would not harm a fly" Others will say, "I have lost all my faith in God, for He cannot be a God of love to ignore my prayers and let my mother die." I do not envy the task of the priest trying to give a satisfying answer, or seeking those platitudinous clichés to meet the occasion. The mourners who know of the truth of continued life are more easily comforted. They know their dear one is freed from all pain and stress on the entry into the larger life, and that in the fullness of time a reunion will take place.

Doctors have tried to account for the success in healings by attributing a sense of faith and expectancy in the sick to be healed. They say that sufferers will come *expecting* to be healed and are therefore ready to accept suggestions from the healer that they are better. This, of course, implies that sick people do not attend their doctors anticipating that they will get well, or that they have lost their faith in the doctors because they have not responded to medical treatment. There may be some truth in this, that patients do come to a healer expecting to receive practical help. But all the anticipation and faith cannot heal or remove a cause of disease. This can only arise from the ordered administration of a planned intelligent process.

Next to faith comes the medical explanation that healings simply follow "suggestion." Naturally, the healer will look for improvement and seek it. Let us consider the locked joint from arthritis. After seeking the dispersal of the holding adhesions, the healer will look to see the extent of the loosening that has been effected. He will gently suggest to the patient to let the limb move to see the full extent of the freedom that has come to the joint. Needless to say, if the looseness has not been attained all the suggestion in the world cannot get it to move.

I recall the story of the healing of a case of blindness. I will quote this from the words printed in *The British Medical Journal* of December 4th, 1954: "Mr. J.E.E. In June, 1952 (after having received spiritual healing) I suddenly recovered the sight in my right eye, which had been completely blind for over fifty years. It came as long sight and was pronounced by the specialist optician as perfect and the healing was miraculous. He observed, 'Vision perfect, eye clear, bright and in splendid condition, no fear of deleterious effects'. The opthalmologist concerned commented: 'There is no miracle—he was a case of spontaneous dislocation of the lens which was cataractus. The lens dislocated back into his vitreous chamber, which is the old operation of couching, and it is brought about by some violent exercise or some sudden jerk. Could there have been functional blindness after the couching which was relieved by suggestion, the patient beginning to see after being encouraged to look'?".

Believe it or not, the suggestion was seriously put forward in the official organ of the British Medical Association that after being blind for fifty years the eye regained its sight on our suggestion that he could see with it. The vision was obscured by a cataract, the lens dislocated for half a century, but all we had to do was to suggest he could see and he could. It is pertinent to ask: "Why did not the opthalmologists tell the man to look and recover his sight—they had fifty years to do this in?" The plain admitted fact is that when the man came to the Sanctuary for the healing of his sight it was restored. This could have become possible only by the dispersal of the cataract and the lens adjusted to enable the eye to become clear and bright with perfect vision. Clearly it was not faith or suggestion that restored the vision but a result arising from the planned intention to remove the causes of the blindness.

Thus "spiritual healing" is far removed from "faith healing". The latter term should never be used in connection with healing from Spirit.

CHAPTER THIRTEEN

HEALING ORGANIC DISEASES

Some medical people admit freely that spiritual healing is able to help neurotic and mental troubles, but they are unwilling to accept that it can cure organic diseases and their effects. This attitude of mind arises from a prejudice which ignores the facts.

These facts are that within our experience there is no disease or affliction that cannot be helped to a greater or lesser extent or completely cured through healing. The only condition that seems to defy the healing is that of fingers which become bent over through tendon tightening.

Infectious diseases, especially tuberculosis, yield to spiritual healing, often very rapidly. Internal disorders, growths of all kinds, paralyses and structural deformities can all respond to the healing effort. Broken limbs, burnings, varicose ulcers, disease and weakness of the organs of sense, they too can be healed.

That is the comprehensive claim which is supported by detailed evidence in thousands of cases and by medical acknowledgments. If I were asked how many patients suffering from organic disabilities we have been instrumental in healing, I could not reply for the number is so vast that we have lost count by thousands. During the past ten years I have received an average of nearly three quarters of a million letters each year from sick people or on behalf of them. When I first commenced absent healing, I received perhaps a score of letters a week. These gradually grew until when I opened Burrows Lea as my healing sanctuary the numbers had arisen to about a thousand a week. Since then the increase has been consistent. Last year the actual number of healing letters amounted to 673,445. By far the greater number of these letters is concerned with the healing of organic troubles. This remarkable growth in the demand for absent healing can only have been achieved by success, often with the healing of the "incurable." If there had not been this considerable measure of success the requests for healing would have waned and died away. Instead of this, the successes attributable to spiritual healing have become so general that the work of the Sanctuary has become household knowledge.

This not only applies to the United Kingdom. Requests for healing arrive from all parts of the world, except those countries behind the Iron Curtain. Last year we purchased from the post office over 70,000 air mail letters for replies.

On most weeks of the year patients arrive at the Sanctuary on four afternoons each week, when, with the good help of my co-operating healers, Olive and George Burton, I conduct three healing sessions and Mr. and Mrs. Burton take the fourth. In this way, between five and six thousand make the journey to Shere every year. During the twelve years the Sanctuary has been open some sixty to seventy thousand sick people have been helped. With their friends and visitors the number of people who have made the journey must be well over one hundred thousand. This, again, is a testimony to success. People who come for healing generally have travelled from all parts of the British Isles and others from very long distances, from the ends of the earth. We have visitors from New Zealand, Australia, Canada, the U.S.A., South Africa and the European continent.

The demand for appointments for contact healing is so great that only a small percentage of applicants can be seen. The method of selection is simple: those who are chosen come from the classification of diseases of a physical kind that are most likely to benefit from contact healing. Almost all of these are of an organic nature. Patients who are suffering from mental troubles and certain kinds of neuroses respond best to absent healing and these are not given priority.

This is *prima facie* evidence that through spiritual healing organic diseases are successfully treated. It must be apparent to the most sceptical minded that the growth of spiritual healing in recent years shows that there is a supernormal beneficent power available in this world to-day.

So far, I have only written of our own work at Shere, but it must not be forgotten that there are thousands of other healers at work in the United Kingdom who maintain their missions in churches and in their homes. It can be stated without fear of contradiction that all these healers have witnessed the healing balm reach their patients, otherwise they would not carry on and sufferers would not go to them.

Some two years ago an effort was made to unify the healing movement, and the National Federation of Spiritual Healers was formed. To-day, its membership exceeds the two thousand mark, and it is steadily growing. The work of healing is carried out voluntarily. In the great majority of cases no fees of any kind are made. At Shere we have never made a charge for healing. The costs of the work and upkeep of the Sanctuary have been met by free-will donations given in gratitude for the healing. The motive behind spiritual healing is that of love and service to one's fellow-man in the name of the Father of us all. It is commonly felt that if any attempt is made to commercialise healing then the gift will suffer. Healing cannot be bought. Another reason why no specific charges are made is that if this were done, it might debar those who are poorly in worldly wealth, the old-age pensioner and the lonely sick who have no income. At Shere, there are "standing orders" to tell those—when it becomes known that to send a donation would be a burden—not to do so.

The reader should be able to assess the total good that healing brings to people, and mainly for the overcoming of organic disabilities. It can be judged that the strength of spiritual healing in the United Kingdom to-day is so strong that it has no need to fear the opposition of any vested interest. It is enthroned within the homes of the people where happiness has been restored in seeing the sick made well.

It will now serve a useful purpose to consider how the healing comes for the relief of the main classifications of disease.

About two years ago, the nation was in the grip of "Asian Influenza". The people of this land did not suffer so severely as in other countries, but it became so prevalent that many factories and schools were closed. Happily we were told in advance by some months of the approaching scourge, and so we were able to make preparations. Through our magazine *The Spiritual Healer* and in all our replies to the letters, we sought the co-operation of people in an effort to prevent infection. We interceded for protection for all the sick and others under our care. We asked for information, firstly to be immediately informed if the symptoms of "Asian 'Flu" were noted and to tell us whenever it affected our people. The result was that, from the information we received, it was a rare occurrence to learn that one of our patients, was a victim, even in those areas, especially in the Midlands, where the epidemic was strongest.

The national percentage of people who had visited doctors for treatment for this virulent type of influenza was fifteen. The percentage of the thousands of people under our care was a fraction of one per cent. One school headmistress wrote for protection for her scholars. While every other school in the area was closed hers remained open and very few scholars were infected. This may seem a fantastic story, yet it is true, and indicates a facet of healing that may not yet be fully appreciated, its function as a preventitive of disease, which will later be explained in fuller detail.

To a lesser degree, the testimony is frequently given that a patient, who hitherto had been allergic to colds and would experience a very bad winter, came through it well and with no colds.

Tuberculosis is another infectious disease that readily yields to spiritual healing. It is only the exceptional case where consistent and marked progress is not dated by the commencement of the healing. The first sign we look for in the reports is that the temperature has come down to normal, and next that the tests prove to be negative, indicating that the infection has been overcome. After this comes a period of convalescence, in which the physical strength is built up and weight increases. The rapidity with which a patient gets better sometimes arouses the doctor's suspicions. For example: the X-rays may denote one or more cavities in the lungs before healing commences; after its intervention, the next X-ray photographs show that the cavities do not appear on the plates, or their structure has so altered that they resemble scar tissue. It can be understood that doctors are puzzled. On a number of occasions they have conducted tonographic and still more intense forms of exploration in an effort to find the cavities. I remember on one occasion the perplexed doctor said, "Well, all I can say is that it must have gone into hiding."

The way in which tuberculosis yields to healing illustrates the advantage that would come from co-operation between the doctor and the healer. The doctor would learn to expect the good changes as we do. I recall cases where, after these supernormal healings occurred, and because the doctors could not understand how the change had taken place, they persisted in continuing the full programme of treatment originally prescribed—and, at times, drastic operations were still carried out as "precautionary measures." Another example is when a lung has shown a cavity and it has been collapsed, air refills were given regularly to maintain the collapsed condition.

When, with the healing, X-ray photographs no longer show the presence of the cavity, we learn sometimes that doctors are not content to accept the evidence of the camera, and insist on maintaining the lung in its collapsed state for the prescribed period, possibly for two more years. If the patients or their relatives had always told the doctors that spiritual healing had been sought, there would have accrued such a mass of supporting evidence that any medical man would have been compelled to take some notice of the fact. Unfortunately the great majority of people seem to be afraid of telling their doctors about spiritual healing, for they fear the medical reaction. This may well be a reflection on the medical profession, for it does seem that people hold them in awe and fear.

They are afraid of being bullied and treated with sarcasm. There was a time when policemen were feared by people and there used to be the parental threat to erring children that the parents "would tell the policeman." This threat would have little importance to-day, for the police are friends with the children as well as with grown-ups. They are no longer feared but thought of as helpful friends.

It would be a much happier position for all concerned if doctors could be regarded in a similar light, but unfortunately it is not always so. Often healers hear the statement from a patient, "I am afraid to go to the doctor for fear he will send me to hospital or suggest an operation." We try to counteract this idea, and repeatedly advise patients to seek the help that doctors can give.

The prevalence of that disease of civilisation, poliomyelitis, gives great concern. Many people are said to contract this disease in a mild form which is soon mastered. It is not yet ascertained what the ultimate value of inoculation with the various vaccines will be, but it is surely morally wrong for humans to benefit from the agonising deaths of hundreds of thousands of our lesser brethren —the monkey—every year. Spiritual healers, as a rule, are not called in until the infection has become firmly established, or to remove the weaknesses resulting from it, sometimes of a number of years' standing. When our help has been sought for patients who are suspected polio cases it has invariably been found that the disease does not develop. The writer is aware that there is no proof of healing in this, but the fact should be recorded. When the presence of the disease is established, and it is not chronic, the removal of the infection soon follows the healing effort and, what is important, without the ill-effects of paralysis.

Then there are those extreme cases where the disease has obtained a firm hold on the patient and the continuance of life is threatened, the patient being kept within an oxygen tent or an iron lung. With these extreme cases, the percentage of success is not high. Yet we do see recoveries take place that are contrary to medical expectation. Were there is liaison in a practical way be-

The two pictures illustrate the healing story. A totally stiffened leg freed at knee and hip

Rayfael

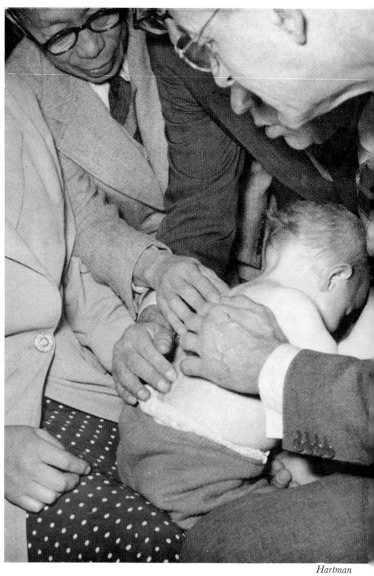

Hartman

Three doctors examine a child's spine after a curvature has been corrected

tween doctor and healer we should make considerable progress in the prevention and cure of this disease without the need for the horrible practices that are perpetrated "in the name of humanity" on monkeys and other animals.

With other forms of infectious troubles, such as gastric afflictions, blood disease, septic and gangrenous sores, spirit healing is effective. We understand that whenever possible the healing guides are able to isolate the affected areas, and to mobilise, through the body intelligence, the resistance in the blood and glands to overcome the viruses and other forms of invaders. The guides also have the ability to impart disrupting forces that can change the chemical atomic elements that go to build up the structures of the germs and so destroy them.

There is no rigid dividing line between one form of healing and another. Thus the processes that go towards the mastering of infections are applicable to the healing of other diseases, of which one is cancer.

In considering the healing of cancer, it is well to recall that causes must first be overcome before a recovery can be established. Cancer research has been going on for fifty years. Two million animals have died as the result of experiments, and yet the cause of cancer has not been discovered. Lord Horder, chairman of the British Empire Cancer Campaign, said: "The essential cause of cancer is still elusive ... the problem was still the problem of the causation of cancer ... the essential causation of cancer in a woman's breast or in a man's stomach still eludes us". Unfortunately the position is still the same to-day.

In 1955, I wrote: "The causation of cancer lies in particularised forms of emotional and spiritual unrest, or disharmony within the inner-self of the person that promotes the glandular turmoil from which the cancer comes." I also wrote: "In almost every case of breast cancer there will be found mental stresses, such as aversion to sex, the wish for children, the desire to avoid children, not wanting children when they come and unpleasant and unhealthy relationships (often maternal)."

In the U.S.A., investigations have been taking place on these lines, and confirmation of my thesis has been established. In a Chicago hospital forty women who had been operated upon for breast cancer were carefully studied. The report states, in words almost identical to mine, that the women "were found to have a similar personality and behaviour. They had an aversion to sex, most of them did not want to have children, they had an unpleasant relationship with their mothers that they covered up with an outward show of sweetness."

Here is a further extract from the same report: "The vast majority of sufferers with leukemia are adults. After numerous and intimate contacts with leukemia patients, it was found that most of them had had harrowing lives."

In this country a number of our leading physicians are now expressing the same point of view. Sir Heneage Ogilvie made the classic statement that "a happy man never gets cancer."

The conclusion can therefore be considered that because cancer has its causation in the disharmony of the human spirit-self it can be effectively treated on the same plane of activity that it exists; that is through spiritual healing. Such disturbances cannot be removed clinically.

Thus it is established: The healing purpose is primarily preventitive, as will be more fully explained later; it overcomes the causes of inner-self distress that creates the cancer; and finally it overcomes and disperses the cancer. The process of dispersal is probably the same as is applied to other forms of growth, such as tumours, cysts, fibroids, goitres, etc.

Many stories could be told of the healing of third-degree malignant cancers where, according to the medical outlook, the condition was hopeless. Typical of these is the story of a postman who was within twelve months of retiring age. He had always been in good health, but suddenly and without warning he felt acute abdominal pain. He was taken to hospital and the surgeon opened him up for an investigation. It was then seen he had an advanced cancerous condition with extensive infiltrations, too severe for operation. He was sewn up. Spiritual healing was sought for him.

He not only recovered from the operation effects but all symptoms of the cancer also disappeared. His local doctor was informed of the surgeon's report, and therefore held no other opinion than that the man must die. The doctor therefore called daily to give him morphine injections. When the son told the doctor that his father had received spiritual healing and was no longer in any pain, that the swelling of the abdomen had reduced and he was putting on weight, and therefore there was no need for the morphia, the doctor's reply was fatalistic. He said: "He has got to die anyway and it may as well be from morphine poisoning as from painful cancer."

In my review of cancer healing, when I prepared my book *The Evidence for Spirit Healing*, I published citations from no less than 281 cases of supernormal results in the healing of growths within a period of four years. That was in 1953. Since then the good record has been not only maintained but healings have become more frequent, as its quality has improved with wisdom, experience and usage.

One method of dispersal of cancer has already been shown in Chapter 9 dealing with "The Healing Forces," in which the dispersing process takes place through the administering by the guides of a disrupting force that breaks up the atomic formation of the elements necessary for the maintainance of life in the disease cells. In these cases the removal of the cancer is generally rapid. A second method was also mentioned, that of dissociating the disease cells from the rest of the healthy body tissue and passing them out of the body through the excretory systems and through vomiting. It is a pity that, on every occasion but one, the stools have been disposed of before any analysis could take place. In the one exception it was established that the stool was composed of a form of "disintegrated tissue," which confirms our view of the healing process. With other patients there has been a very excessive amount of perspiration in the armpits and with the feet. This profuse perspiration continues for some days, creating a very tender and sore condition. With this, the symptoms of the cancer have disappeared.

A more general way in which cancers are observed to go is by its gradual dissolution. This is the usual manner with breast cancers. It is a common experience with contact healing for breast cancer for the healer to feel the change in the density of the growth It becomes softer and smaller in size, it becomes malleable and "floating". When this is followed by absent healing the dispersal progressively continues until it disappears. By this means it is assumed that the substance of the cancer is gradually but progressively broken down, dispersed through the blood and carried away. We do not see successful healings in every case, but the number where the trouble vanishes is considerable.

One doctor whom I tried (unsuccessfully) to interest in the healing of cancer summarily dismissed the results, saying the cancers were not cancers at all but were only cysts or swellings from mastitis and that his contemporaries had made wrong diagnoses. (It is noteworthy how doctors are prone to alter their diagnosis when, through healing, the cancers have been dispersed, and how they are willing to prejudice the reputation of their colleagues by imputing wrong diagnosis to them.) Incidentally, he agreed with me that in numbers of cases where operations had taken place to remove the whole or part of the breast (where a mass of substance had been diagnosed as cancer) they were unnecessary, for they were probably not cancers.

With abdominal cancers the healer is able to see in contact healing the breaking down and lessening of tension and swelling, as the dispersing process takes place.

Whether spiritual healing is able to bring about a recovery or not is an individual one. Whereas we sometimes see an advanced cancerous state very quickly healed in a supernormal manner, it must be said that this is the exception rather than the rule. When a cancer is treated in its early stages the percentage of healings is much greater.

Unfortunately, cases are mostly only brought to the healer's notice when the cancer is far advanced and the bodily vitality has become very low. No food can be accepted, the resistance and vitality are at a very low ebb and the days of life are numbered.

We do not witness a recovery in the majority of such cases, but the sick one is helped, more than words can tell. Dating from the healing, the patient loses his sense of pain and stress, he sleeps peacefully and the passing is easy and quite free from the agony usually associated with malignant cancers.

Leukemia is said to be cancer of the blood and, medically speaking, there is no cure. With adults the degree of ultimate success is low, but there is mounting evidence to indicate that the life of the patient has been sustained without undue stress for a period of years. Greater success is observed with children who contract this disease. At the time of writing there are a number of boys and girls who have made wonderful recoveries, but we cannot say yet whether a cure has been affected, for it is understood that regressions are liable to occur. Here is a quotation from a recent letter: "My son has been very well and full of life. He saw the specialist to-day—once again he is very delighted with him. His blood count was 110. All the doctors are very pleased with him. They have lost every case here of leukemia since my boy started it twenty months ago and most of them only lived twelve weeks, with the exception of one boy who lived five months. Surely if any credit is due to the drugs, then some other child would have responded as well as my son."

I would like to tell the story of a leukemia healing—I supplied the case history to the Archbishops' Commission. This history commenced in September, 1952, but we will go to the crucial date of December 13 when a doctor at a London hospital diagnosed that a boy was suffering from a type of leukemia usually found in adults. It was quite incurable. The boy was transferred to another hospital and placed under the care of one of the hospital's specialists.

On December 16 the boy's father had an interview with the doctor, who confirmed the diagnosis of chronic myeloid leukemia. He told the father there was no hope of recovery. He could try deep X-ray treatment, but this would only cause the boy unnecessary suffering. The remission, if any, would be dearly bought and could only defer the inevitable end.

This was the state of the case on December 16. The boy's condition was thought to be totally hopeless. On December 17 the boy's father met a friend who told him about spiritual healing and with the father's permission wrote to me for absent healing. This letter was received on December 18 and absent healing commenced that day.

December 19. This is the critical day to be noted. From this day the boy began to get better. The doctor told the father that at 4 p.m. he noted that "something different" had taken place with the lad, and a mild X-ray treatment was given.

From December 19 to the end of the year progress continued, with the boy receiving *sun-ray* treatment. On January 11 the white cell count was down to half what it had previously been. On January 24 the boy was able to go home. The improvement with the blood count was consistent until normality was achieved. On March 10 the boy returned to school. At each monthly checkup at the hospital the blood count was found to be normal and so it continued throughout the year of 1953, and onwards.

When it was known that this case had been sent for investigation to the Archbishops' Commission, the doctor sent for the parents and advised them that the period of remission was running out, and that if there was a relapse little or no hope could be given that the boy would again respond to "X-ray treatment." It should be noted that the doctor, while knowing about the spiritual healing, preferred to attribute the boy's recovery to the X-ray treatment. He told the parents that there was no medical record of recovery from this disease. There were one or two exceptional cases of two, and still more rarely three years' remission following deep X-ray treatment. He said he would think the boy was in the exceptional class if he reached safely to three years' immunity, but on medical experience he expected a relapse after two years and after that his life might not last more than six months.

Is is now seven years and the boy is well. A leading authority on blood diseases who reviewed the case, said any discrepancy in the blood count can now be ignored.

When a person has back and leg pains it has become the fashion to diagnose slipped discs. This is an advance on the previous diagnoses that were content with describing the affliction as lumbago, sciatica, fibrositis or rheumatism, etc., and treatment was applied to the symptoms and not the cause. Healers have been more conscious that the causes of these painful conditions arise in the spinal column. A very common cause is that a spastic condition, or stiffening of the vertebræ, most often in the lumbar region and behind the shoulders and in the neck, has arisen which is often described as "slipped disc" when indeed it is not. To many healers the freeing of the vertebræ and the re-alignment of spines where there is a maladjustment or even a slipped disc is usually a very simple matter. As the healer places his hands over the affected spine, and seeks the loosening of the adhesions, so the spine yields and flexibility returns. As this is accomplished, the pressures on the emerging nerves that branch out from in between each section of the backbone are removed and the symptoms of pain in the back and legs soon vanish.

Healers welcome medical co-operation, but there does exist a fundamental difference of opinion between healers and doctors on the treatment of joints that are painful and set. The doctors recommend immobility, and in many cases suggest this with rheumatism and arthritis as well as with spinal conditions. The patient is kept bedfast and no movement is allowed. The result is that every opportunity is given for the adhesions to increase, sometimes so ossifying the joints that they never move again. True, further pain in the joint is prevented, but this is not healing. Spiritual healers are convinced that the better way of treating these conditions is to disperse the adhesions and, maintaining all possible movements gently and without force, seek still further loosening to come, encouraging the joints to take advantage of the induced looseness. Of course no pressure or force is ever used— no one can heal by force—there must be a yielding of the trouble as beneficial changes come. Moreover, with healing, there is no pain, not even with the agonising condition of slipped disc or joints tortured with arthritic crystals.

When the doctors think a manipulation is advisable, such as with an arm or leg, the patient must first be rendered unconscious by an anæsthetic, otherwise the pain would be too excruciating to bear. With spiritual healing there should be no pain at all; the joint or spine yields as the obstructions are dispersed. I have treated many thousands of severely painful joints and it is very rarely that sufferers feel even a twinge of pain. Psychology plays a part in this. When patients attend for medical treatment they expect to be hurt, and doctors and nurses become innured to causing pain. But when these same patients receive spiritual healing, they do so knowing that the healer will not cause them to suffer, and therefore relinquish themselves to the healing, relaxing the body and the limbs. They "give themselves" to the healer, without contracting and restricting the muscles.

In public healing services, when a patient comes on to the platform with an obvious chronic condition of arthritis, the hands are knotted. The sufferer can only hobble along with assistance, and the arms can hardly move. It is invariably seen that, through the gentle administration of the healing, looseness returns until the arms can be moved freely upwards and in all directions. The wrists become supple and the fingers are able to bend. The hip joints are freed and the patient can lift the knee in a goose-step movement. When this takes place, as part of the demonstration I may ask two questions. The first is: "When were you able to move your limbs like this before?" The usual answer is: "It's so long ago that I cannot remember." The second question is: "What would happen if anyone else moved your limb like this?" Again the usual answer is: "I would have screamed out in pain."

Returning to the spine itself, it is often apparent, owing to the length of time the patient has suffered, that the vertebræ have become solid—what is called "poker-back." This implies that the cushioning discs between the joints have sadly deteriorated and may hardly be there at all. It is one of the mysteries of spirit healing that when freedom of movement is restored to a poker-back condition, there is no pain or grating sounds as the joints palpate one with another. The inference is that with the dispersal of the obstructing substances, the intervertebræ discs are restored into function at the same time.

Spinal curvatures, sometimes existing from childhood, or at times from birth, or from results from weakening diseases like polio and disseminated sclerosis, also yield to healing. If the curvature is a mild one it may instantly respond. If the curvature is severe, like a pronounced letter "S" with the lumbar spine bending right out to one side and the dorsal spine bent out under the shoulder blade, it will need a series of treatments progressively to restore alignment. Needless to say, such conditions are considered to be totally incurable by the medical profession.

In order to show doctors the comparative ease with which spinal troubles, such as slipped discs and spastic conditions yield to spiritual healing, an invitation was sent to the British Medical Association. They were asked to arrange for a number of patients suffering from these troubles to be assembled and a number of healers would be invited to come and demonstrate the healing processes. The reason why a number of healers would attend was to show that the healing of spines is a general practice and not the result of a special gift with only one. It is suggested that no harm could come from this experiment as the healing would take place in the presence of doctors, but possibly much good. Needless to say this invitation has not been accepted. One is entitled to ask, "Why?" Probably, as a matter of professional policy, the British Medical Association refuses even to consider the healing potential as expressed through healers.

In the case of slipped disc, the medical procedure is usually to admit the patients into hospital. There they are kept immobile for a month or more, hoping that the spine will readjust itself, which it rarely can do because it is denied the function of movement. After this the patient has to undergo traction treatment which involves pulling the spine by attaching weights through pulleys to the legs and head. Here again the percentage of success is small. Then if the patient's spine has not yielded to these or osteopathic manipulations the surgeon comes into the picture. He either cuts away the ligament protrusions or grafts a piece of bone alongside the backbone in the form of a splint to prevent the spine moving at all; and, lastly, to provide an unyieldable spinal jacket with steel stays and structure to prevent the patient moving his back at all and so preventing pain. Obviously, these final procedures are not healing ones but capitulation to the condition.

The ease with which severe spinal troubles yield to healing may be gathered from the two following examples which I purposely include for two reasons; one is they were submitted to the Archbishops' Commission and were offered for investigation to the British Medical Association's special committee appointed for the purpose and, secondly, to prove the permanence of spirit healing.

The first case is that of Mr. William Olsen, who suffered from a spinal collapse with slipped discs. He was admitted to hospital and underwent the usual treatments as already described, but without avail. His condition deteriorated, he was in continual agony, could not sleep or eat, became wasted and paralysis was becoming obvious. Finally with his whole body encased in plaster he was sent home, uncured, but given drugs to ease the pain. Owing to the agony he got his wife and son to saw off the plaster covering. The next morning (it happened to be Christmas Day) he was assisted into a car and driven to the Sanctuary. I gently sought for the realignment of the spine. Within three minutes this was accomplished. Mr. Olsen could stand upright, and bend over to touch his toes. All pain had vanished. He went home to enjoy his Christmas fare after a long, peaceful and refreshing sleep. The Archbishop's Commission asked for medical acknowledgment of his recovery and this Mr. Olsen was unable to obtain. I therefore sought the aid of the British Medical Association to conduct further enquiries and eventually they arranged for him to be interviewed by the same hospital surgeon who had had charge of his case. The surgeon testified that the healing was complete, but he would not comment upon the part that spirit healing had played in the recovery, for it had happened eighteen months earlier.

Since the three minutes healing on that Christmas Day in 1953 Mr. Olsen has had no trouble whatsoever.

The second case is that of a woman who in childhood contracted a spinal curvature that produced progressively worsening symptoms. For forty years she was under hospital and medical care without any benefit. Instead the curvature became a hunchback. The X-ray photographs showed (and I quote from the medical report): "Dorsal spine: — There is gross kyphosis on the level DV 4, 5 and 6 with partial destruction and wedging of 3, 4 and 5. There may be some soft paravertebral tissue swelling associated with this. The appearances are of old-Potts disease. Lumbar Spine and Pelvis: — C.A. Changes are present in the lower lumbar spine and there would appear to be some narrowing of the disc spaces V4 and 5 and LV 5 and S1." As time passed, her condition continued to deteriorate. She was in continual pain, paralysis came to the legs and she could only slowly hobble about with the aid of two sticks, with her body bent right over. This was her condition after forty years' medical treatment. She then came to the Sanctuary. Once more the adjusting treatment lasted only from three to five minutes. The result was that she was able to stand upright, her hunchback position disappeared, her spine was centred, and she was free from pain. She discarded her sticks and could walk normally. From that day in 1951 she has had no trouble. It is interesting to note that other weaknesses, such as with her vision, have also gone. Since then she has married and is an active farmer's wife. In gratitude for her treatment she opened her home as a healing sanctuary.

The medical committee, dealing with her case, did not call her before them to examine the facts. Nor did they ask for her medical history or for the X-ray plates that showed her condition before the healing and those taken afterwards.

When paralysis has ensued after spinal injuries, sometimes following lumbar injections, or nerve disease, such as with poliomyelitis, or from the ill-effects of numbing pressures on the nerves as with disseminated sclerosis, the healing is often able to restore the co-ordination and control of function. As a rule this takes time,

especially when there is tissue wastage. It is clear that the health
state of the nerve cells must be invigorated for this to happen.
We always seek the co-operation of the patient gently to sustain
the directive for movement through mental anticipation, to encourage the nerves to carry the message from the brain down
through the nerves to obtain the muscular response. We advise a
similar practice with all forms of paralysis, such as with the ill-
effects resulting from "strokes," cerebral haemorrhages, etc.

As we have indicated with the healing of leukemia, the circulation can be stimulated, weaknesses overcome, and even the con-
stituents of the bloodstream corrected. This has been recorded
with blue babies. While success is not always seen there are cases
where these babies have been restored contrary to the medical
prognosis.

I would like to tell two stories to illustrate this. There was a
blue baby, only a few weeks old. She was so weak that doctors
could not give a blood transfusion. The parents were told their
baby could not live and would die at any hour. Our help was sought
by telephone and we interceded by absent healing. Within a matter
of hours a change was noted in the baby. She had new strength.
In the words of the doctor in charge at a London hospital, where
the baby was, "it appeared she had come into a new life." The
blood content began to change and the blueness progressively
went. Thus the change from the hopeless condition to the better
was dated by the commencement of spirit healing. There is a
sequel to this story. When the doctors observed the change, they
gave a "new" drug. Because the baby fully recovered, the hospital
authorities made a memorandum of the case, giving the history
and details of treatment by the new drug. This memorandum was
circulated to other hospitals so they might do likewise.

Before I give the second story I should mention that, in numbers of cases, where a supernormal result has followed spirit healing, the patients have been considered "exhibition cases." Their
case histories, with treatment, have been circulated or they have
been presented before panels of experts as exceptional cases for

review. Usually the doctors were not aware that spiritual healing had intervened. When it was known this factor was ignored. It is suggested that when there are a number of supporting cases with a particular disease that can rule out coincidence or spontaneous recovery, the doctors will be able to recognise and anticipate the characteristic changes associated with patients receiving spirit healing and co-operation between doctors and healers will be effective. Until that time comes the doctors are liable to place more importance upon a drug or treatment than is warranted and thereby may mislead themselves and their contemporaries.

The second case, testifying to the healing of the very young with circulation and other complications, follows a telephone request by a father. He asked if I would go to a Guildford hospital, to baptise his baby who was expected to pass on at any minute. As a recognised Spiritualist minister of religion, I went to the hospital accompanied by Mrs. Burton to baptise the dying child. We were taken into the babies ward, where a dozen or more newly arrived little ones lay in their cots. Ours was in an oxygen tent. She was blue, suffering from convulsions, could not take any nourishment and was very weak. The mother, also ill, was wheeled into the nursery in a chair and the sister in charge also came. The oxygen tent was opened to enable me to place my hand within and perform the ceremony of baptism. As I did so, I intuitively had a strong conviction that the baby would live. In a short talk with the father and mother, who believed in spiritual healing I was able to comfort them without making any forecast. From that time, the baby never had a further convulsion. The colour changed from blue to the natural pink and she soon accepted nourishment. Within one day the change was so noticeable that the doctors told the parents that danger had passed. Incidentally the mother also lost her sickness. The baby is now a charming little girl and perfectly healthy.

There may be good reasons why babies and young children respond readily to healing. They are uninhibited, have no conscious fears like adults possess, and are receptive to the healing.

The little bodies are not set and owing to the malleable condition are able to react quickly to the healing forces sent by the guides.

With functional diseases such as diabetes and glandular ill-conditions, healings are not as a rule rapid. It appears in these cases that time is needed to induce the corrective changes to re-order the function of the body systems, to overcome the cause and the symptoms that follow. Some circulatory conditions come within this proviso. Varicose troubles, pernicious anæmia and jaundice yield gradually yet progressively to the healing forces. This is understandable. Whereas we see a more rapid healing when obstructive substances can be freely dispersed, functional weaknesses need more time to induce the corrective chemical changes to the system so as to strengthen the rightful functioning of the cells. In healings of these types, the only logical explanation is that by the introduction of the lacking qualities that the cells need to bring them into a healthy and purposeful state the beneficial change is induced. This has already been noted in the restitution of the normal quantities of the red blood cells in leukemia and with blue babies.

I recall that when I appeared before the Archbishops' Commission and mentioned this manner of healing, one doctor categorically denied its possibility. I am reminded of the medical attitude to Sir Herbert Barker. For many years he was referred to as a "quack" by the medical profession and his anæsthetist was struck off the medical register. In later years Sir Herbert lectured on his methods to the eminent physicians of that time—from which arose the growth of orthopædic treatment in common use to-day.

Concerning the restoration of the senses, notably with sight and hearing, considerable success is noted, not only with the repairing of organic deficiencies and the overcoming of disease but also with the restoration of function caused through nerve depreciation.

Two recent instances come to mind possessing a similarity with both sight and hearing, to illustrate the power of the healing to redress long-standing weaknesses. At the Central Hall, West-minster, a retired clergyman of the Church of England came to the platform wondering if the waning hearing in his right ear could be strengthened. He was not concerned about his left ear, for that had been stone deaf for thirty years. Healing strength was sought. When he was tested it was discovered that he had regained the sense of hearing in the stone deaf ear and could even hear a whisper in it. The hearing in the right ear was so much better that when he put back his hearing aid conversation sounded like shouting. When this clergyman reported some time later that the good results had been maintained, he volunteered the information that his rheumatism had also disappeared.

The second case relates to the wife of a Methodist minister who came to the Sanctuary for healing. One purpose was to seek clearer vision for her right eye. The left one had not been able to record sight for thirty years. Mrs. Burton treated her, and when she took her hands away it was seen that a comparable degree of sight had come back to the near-blind eye.

Mrs. Burton is used for the healing of sight, hearing and nerve and mind troubles. It has been ascertained over the years that she is employed more effectively by the guides for these special pur-poses. Thus it becomes apparent that some healers are more attuned or adaptable instruments then others for treating specific diseases. This leads to further speculation.

It is obvious that no one spirit guide can possess all the know-ledge relating to healing any more than an earthly doctor can know everything about all human ill-conditions and therapy—that is why we have specialists. It appears, therefore, that there are "specialists in spirit" who have more closely studied one aspect of healing and the law-governed forces concerned with it than other guides. Therefore the guides best suited to deal with par-ticular diseases are called upon by the spirit organisation associated with any individual healer to take over the treatment. The implication also follows that some healers are found by cer-tain guides to be more easily used for the healing purpose than others.

The diseases and ill-conditions associated with both sight and hearing are many. While the percentage of success in healing with them is variable, experience has shown that no limit should be previously imposed by the healer upon the facility with which conditions affecting the senses can respond to the healing. Those cases where the cause of a weakening sense is due to a slackening in the functioning of the optic and aural nerves to carry the message to the consciousness respond best of all. Experience has proved that by energising these nerves receptivity is increased. When this weakening is due to advanced age the healing may not be able to restore full functioning, but in many cases the senses have been strengthened and further depreciation stayed.

Conjunctivitis in all its forms is yieldable, so are cataracts and glaucoma. In some cases even detached retinas have been corrected. From the records it is shown that where surgery has taken place the percentage of success is less, and indeed this applies to most organic troubles. The reason for this is obvious. Where there has been an artificial interference with the natural functioning it becomes more difficult to restore. This does not imply any reflection upon the skill of the surgeons. They do wonderful work, yet nevertheless the fact remains. As with most other afflictions when healing is invited, if the trouble is in its infancy the good result more rapidly follows. This particularly applies to cataracts. It is not infrequent that in early cases we see the vision completely cleared, which is substantiated by the ophthalmologist on later examinations.

When hearing is affected by some mechanical difficulty in the middle ear this, as a rule, is rectified. More time is needed for the restoration of perfection when the cause lies in the delicate organisation of the inner ear. Noises are often stubborn, but we do see these progressively lessen in severity. The time gap increases between phases as the nerve tensions that promote the noises are soothed.

The origin of weakened senses and distressing effects we often find to be within the mental state itself, and shocks or continual worries produce the ill-results. In these cases, the disharmonies

(1) Crippled with rheumatoid arthritis, a patient helped up the steps

Rafael

2) After the healing, the atient's hands and feet re much easier and he able to walk with omparative ease and ithout his stick

(3) Note the hand crippled with arthritis. The patient had been afraid to shake hands because of the intense pain

(4) The fingers are freed and the patient is able to grip the healer's hands

within the total minds are first redressed to enable the senses to be freed.

Another major cause of weakening sight is due to exacting close work in the patient's employment, and if this is persisted in then the healing benefit is negatived. It does seem that patients are more willing to sacrifice their eyes rather than make the effort to seek an easier form of employment. Another human difficulty that interferes with healing progress is that patients are reluctant to "nurse" their eyes and so assist the healing in its work of restoration. If one has a bad arm one will nurse it by supporting it in a sling, but with the eyes one continues to use them to the full, and will not miss seeing a television programme. Notwithstanding this, the measure of success in the healing of the senses is considerable.

Ill-conditions that appear to be organic, so far as the effects are felt in the body but which have a purely nervous cause, are dealt with in the next chapter, although seemingly they are solely related to organic function.

In healing practice, there are other factors that can assist or resist the healing, and which may be referred to as obedience to the laws of health and body hygiene. For example, constipation is a prime cause of illness. The bloodstream becomes toxic and is unable to carry out its function of vitalising the cells and carrying on its mission of discharging waste. The family of arthritic and rheumatic complaints may have at times its cause in this way, as well as many gastric afflictions. While the healing can promote a good health state, and so assist with the overcoming of constipation, it is wise for patients to help themselves. We advise patients to carry out the essential laws for good health, to avoid constipation; to breathe fully and take in a full quota of oxygen; to avoid worry and anxiety; to employ abdominal massage to stimulate the intestinal movements, and massage for stimulating the circulation and for the softening of muscular hardnesses as with fibrositis, etc.

The healer not only is the channel through which the actual healing comes but he is also in the position to give good advice to enable the patient to seek the way to co-operate in all good sense with the healing purpose.

9

The author has no detailed medical knowledge. It may be that its possession could prove hampering to a healer, for he is likely to employ his knowledge rather than allow the intuitive directions to reach his mind through his attunement with the guides. A general knowledge of anatomy and the body systems is, of course, helpful, so long as it deals with the mechanism of the body and is not over-concerned with medicines, drugs and so forth. The mind of the healer should be free in attunement to receive diagnosis and instruction. The gift of diagnosis is most useful and generally comes with healing experience, but it is not essential. It must be the function of the guide to assess the trouble and its cause, in order to know what character of treatment, influence and healing force is needed to master the given condition. When the guide is able to impart this diagnosis to the attuned mind of his instrument then the healer has the advantage of consciously co-operating with the healing directive.

While in this chapter only the main classifications of disease have been referred to, this does not mean that other afflictions cannot be helped. Of course they can and we have yet to find a physical disharmony that cannot be healed to a greater or lesser extent, or even completely. Often it is seen that when one trouble is overcome others soon go.

With spiritual healing of the physical body there is a limitless field of opportunity. While no healer is able, of himself, to give any undertaking in advance that a trouble will be removed, he should never limit within his consciousness the power of the Spirit to heal, within the scope of the total laws that govern us all.

CHAPTER FOURTEEN

HEALING NERVOUS DISEASE

In the field of nervous diseases, spirit healing comes into its own. In Chapter 9 on "Healing Forces" and Chapter 13 on "Healing Organic Diseases" the methods have been indicated by which the guides correct weaknesses and remove physical ill-conditions. It should however be borne in mind that the larger percentage of these are the effects arising from a nervous cause. No healing can ever be effective until the cause has been overcome. As the origin of so much disease lies within the disharmonies in the physical and spirit minds, so they come within the category of nervous diseases, as will be shown in some detail.

Why we unfortunately have so many incurable conditions is for the reason that our medical people are unable to ascertain where the cause of the disease originates, its character, and that, so far, it has been outside their abilities to remove it.

When, with spirit healing, we witness the recovery of a declared "incurable" it must indicate that the guides have been able to overcome the cause, thus permitting the symptoms to be mastered. Disease is a result of cause and effect, and it is simple logic that both must be dealt with before a full return to good health can be re-established.

Spirit healing is a progressive process, commencing with the origin and following on with the correction afterwards.

In order to remove a cause, the conditions that create it must be appreciated and understood. It must have a foundation in a state of being, and the changing of this state can only be effected on the same level as it exists. Medical treatments are on the physical plane, dealing with states that surrender to change under the laws pertaining to matter.

Therefore the act of bringing about a corrective change within the minds of a patient can only become operative under conditions of parity and on the same level. The pertinent fact is that, with spirit healing, the primary causes of disease are induced to yield to the remedial influences, for otherwise the sick would not get well.

The seat of all human experience is in the consciousness. This is not an organisation but is the faculty of perception, receiving impressions and experiences from both the physical and the spirit self. Associated with the consciousness are our nerve systems and glandular reactions. The sensitive, functional and motor nerves operate from the consciousness either directly or subconsciously. The nerves that control all our movements receive their orders from it, as likewise do those nerves of function that maintain the heart beats and the digestion. It is the consciousness that registers every feeling and sense. It enables us to associate one thought with another and so create a third. It can recall from the reservoir of experience items of knowledge at will—without it, memory could not function.

It is through the consciousness that our conscience comes, and this introduces the ability to differentiate between right and wrong. It is through the consciousness the conscience possesses the faculty of distinguishing between spiritual and evil intentions, and therefore it is receptive to influence from the spirit or inner-self as well as from the physical mind.

When the consciousness is free from a background of anxiety, we have a feeling of well-being, but when it is harassed and over-taxed it dulls and depresses the outlook. After a period of over-study, the performing of exacting responsibilities, or if it is troubled by a bad conscience, it is unable to appreciate clearly and there is difficulty in clear thinking or absorbing fresh knowledge; it becomes dulled and stale.

When there is an ever-present acute anxiety it creates on the consciousness a background of stress that blankets its perceptiveness and adversely colours the outlook. In this state the nerve and glandular systems are affected, and they, too, suffer from tiredness and inertia. The person feels depleted, and there is no joy in life. It is as if the headquarters loses its intimate and close contact and control. One feels slack and can easily become a prey to depression, so that one's health resistance goes down.

When this condition obtains one becomes more prone to disease and infection. The glandular system that deals with growth, the health of every cell and its reproduction, the emotions, sex and regulation of the body temperatures and processes, becomes dulled. If the cause of the depression is deep-seated and persists for a period of time, so the glandular health continues to decline. It loses its firm control over the purpose and the health of the cells, enabling a renegade cell to overthrow the restraining good direction, to run amok, and so commence a cancer or other trouble. It lays the body open to the invasion of virus. Through the depreciation of vitality in the good health tone of the nerves the bloodstream in its turn becomes weaker and does not function at its best, again laying the body open to all sorts of disease such as arthritis and functional disorders.

Simple evidence to prove this is seen with gastric ulcers. All medical authorities agree that many arise from neuroses. It is the business executive who carries the burden of responsibility who is more prone to gastric ulcers. Most forms of skin trouble, particularly shingles, are directly associated with nervous temperaments and harassed minds. The man or woman who worries over detail and who is fearful in mind, or who has justifiable cause for anxiety, is the one who suffers from migraine and headaches. When a person feels very deeply the loss of a dear one, so that it is ever present in their consciousness, there is seen the reason for a breakdown in health, sometimes very severely. Anæmia and jaundice have the common cause in the undermining of the body resistance and health tone through some form of mind disharmony. So this story can go on and on, and its lessons lead us back to the fundamental cause of disease originating in mental and nervous stress.

It becomes very clear that to circumvent the cause of disease balance and perspective need to be restored to the outlook, nervous tensions must be calmed and soothed. This can be achieved only by the thought processes becoming adjusted. Spiritual healing achieves this, and it is pertinent to ask how and by what means it is able to accomplish it.

Once the truth is admitted that the inner-mind is open to receive influencing from Spirit the answer is easy to see. In physical life, when it is known what the cause of a mental trouble may be, the mind can be comforted by good counsel. This is the practice of psychiatry. It is done every day in common life where friends or relatives will employ all the reasons they can command to show a sufferer from mental sickness how to place the trouble in its right perspective and to give assurances that comfort and restore confidence in right thinking. At times this is not an easy thing to achieve, for it is a fact that such patients may hold on to their miseries and will not accept the good advice of their friends.

It is suggested that the spirit guides are more easily able to direct good influencing, especially when it is remembered that the greater percentage of mental turbulence has its origin in the spirit mind which is the seat of the emotions, character and directive of life's purpose. There is a great difference between physical fear and mental fear; the former belongs to the physical mind, the latter to the spirit mind.

In order to relate our troubles to friends we have to rely upon our ability to express our worries and fears in words which are so inadequate, and at the best this is generally ineffectually done. The spirit people are not so handicapped. The spirit mind is on the same plane as the spirit mind of the guide, who is able to read the patient's mind openly and fully. The guide is able to see the basic cause of the trouble in all its detail, and is able to direct to it those adjusting thoughts to overcome the disharmony. As these are recorded on the consciousness and the physical mind perceives them, so is the way opened for the acceptance of new thoughts that overpower the old distressing ones. Let me give an example.

A woman called at the Sanctuary with her young daughter. She was in an extreme state of tension and it was clear to see that she was mentally distressed. It appeared from her story that she was fearful that something would happen to her little girl, an accident of some sort. She was in a state of mental terror when the daughter was away from her at school. She told me that she had not slept for a long time and it was obvious that a nervous breakdown was near. I gave her comfort and assurances, I sought easement for her mind and for spirit influence to take away her fears. She came again about a week later, simply to give thanks. It was apparent that she was a different person. Her face was smiling and her eyes were happy. I enquired how the good change had come and she told me.

The day following her visit to me she found herself walking towards the school, arriving there at "break time." She stood outside the railings and soon saw her daughter playing happily with her friends. As she stood and watched, she said she felt as if someone was close and talking to her mind. She was asked to look at all the other children, and especially the older ones who had all grown up without anything happening to them. Why should any accident come to her daughter? She felt that there was a guiding presence that gave her mind the assurance that her daughter would be protected from harm. As she realised this she felt a great load lifted from her. She told me that since then she had not been to the school to fetch her daughter home, a habit that had never before been broken.

This story illustrates how a corrective influence was directed with a reasoned sequence of thought to take away her fears. Her feeling that "someone was with her" indicates that the healing took place through her inner-self or spirit self. As her consciousness received this, and her physical mind accepted and appreciated the good advice, so the happy change had come to her outlook.

Here is another example that I now recall. A man in a good position was an alcoholic. There was no lack of money. The wife told me he was a good man and father to his children, but he was addicted to drinking throughout the day. As a rule he would come home the worse for it. While he was not cruel in any way, he seemed to be oblivious of the home, his wife and children. She was worried, for she could see that with the persistence of the drinking habit it was becoming stronger; she feared for her husband's health and that he would "drink himself to death." I told her that we would seek spirit help to reach him. The sequel came in this way.

The man had cause one evening, soon after, to call at the home of a member of his staff. He was invited in and given a welcome. The children made a great fuss of him and he co-operated in their play. As he did this, his conscience drew the comparison with this home and his own. On his way home, he entered a public garden and sat on a seat, something he had never done before. As he sat there pictures came to his mind. He told his wife afterwards that he felt as if he were at the cinema and was looking at actual pictures. These brought back scenes of his earlier married life, of the honeymoon, of holidays and the coming of their first child. He saw himself in the pictures as he used to be, happy and living in the homely atmosphere. He told his wife that he could not draw himself away, he felt glued to the seat, and did not really want to break off the experience. He went straight home. On going in, he felt the looks of apprehension in the eyes of his family and was conscious of the happy change in them when they realised he was his normal self.

As in the previous case, there was given a sequence of thought with purpose behind it, and which was not of his seeking. My last news about the man was that he had taken the lesson so much to heart that he had foresworn drinking alcohol.

There are many stories of this nature. Each is an individual one, pertaining to the personal picture. Two cases have been given in a previous chapter relating to the change in the character of patients that has taken place, and which we have dated by the healing intercession. There are however, other disease-making causes that are not so apparent, and these apply to hidden frustrations within the self. It may be that from childhood the person has an inner desire to follow some art or mission in life, but owing to circumstances and, possibly, parental influence, this yearning has not been fulfilled and he has been forced into another way of life. Even though this has been accepted, there would still remain the underlying dissatisfaction within the spirit self that continues to be rebellious, thus creating a disharmony which can lead to the coming of disease.

To illustrate this, I think of Mr. and Mrs. Burton's eldest son, Roger. From an early age he expressed the desire to serve God as a minister of the Church. When he was at his preparatory school he organised a prayer and devotional group amongst fellow-scholars. They used to meet in a school-room one evening a week. For days beforehand, Roger would write out the prayers and the subjects for study. As may be imagined, this took a great deal of courage, for the rest of the boys were unsympathetic, and not only chaffed them but caused so much upset that the headmaster was forced to disallow the meetings. Yet Roger's purpose continued. When he went to public school, the headmaster advised him to consider well before adopting the Church as a profession in view of the scanty stipends paid, which, he felt, some might think a poor return for the cost of his education. Happily, Roger has been able to continue in the way his heart has been set. Had there been circumstances to prevent this being so, it is not difficult to see how the bitterness of frustration would be with him, opening the door to uncertainty and unrest that would have turned him from a happy vocation into a less satisfying one that he did not want—with its inevitable conclusions.

There are other ways in which the even tenor of a life can be thwarted. I have known of mental and nervous disease that can be traced to a terrifying experience in childhood, such as an attack upon a young girl by a sexual pervert. The wounds such experiences cause on the soul or spirit-self are so deep that they do not heal, and affliction follows. It is only through spiritual healing that the inner-self frustrations and woundings can be healed and physical harmony restored.

There are few other conditions that command sympathy more than those associated with Parkinson's Disease, especially when it comes to a comparatively young man or woman. There is no question that the primary cause for this disease lies in mind stress, overtaxing the mental capabilities or for other reasons, incurring a positive disease of the nerve function. Inertia sets in, accompanied by tremors of the face, body and limbs. We have noted that in all these cases the tremors and spasms go when the patient is asleep. Thus the need is to soothe the nervous tensions, and spirit healing can often do much to remove the distress.

Another conclusion that can be reached is that the spirit guides are able directly to influence the action of the physical nerves. In a very great number of cases of normally extremely painful conditions associated with a disease we see the pains taken away, as for example with cancers, meningitis, etc. When a healer gives contact healing for some agonising trouble, such as rheumatoid arthritis, slipped discs, gout, or internal suffering, no pain is caused while the treatment is taking place and it is greatly lessened or entirely removed afterwards. Every day, reports in cases of absent healing tell the same story, that "the pains have gone." The hypotheses are advanced that these good effects are either produced by direct influence on the nerves at the seat of the trouble and/or the consciousness is influenced not to record the stress. With Parkinson's Disease the healing influences must be able to soothe the nerve tensions and progressively eliminate the tremors. Where there is the complication of inertia or heaviness in movement, a new incentive is directed to the motor nerves to function and co-ordinate with the instructions given by the consciousness.

With all forms of muscular paralysis, whatever the disease may be, whether from stroke, polio, sclerosis, atrophies, etc., progress is seen to a variable degree through healing, sometimes resulting in complete removal of the weakness. These healings take time, implying that the nerve cells need a period of convalescence for them to receive invigoration. There are cases in our records where a nerve has been severed through surgery and the affected part of the body made helpless. Yet with the healing there has come a gradual return of function. This is, of course, beyond all medical expectation. It seems that, in ways known to the healing guides, they are able to establish a link, either directly or by by-passing the severance with other nerve cells, or adjusting the purpose of connecting cells to a different character of purpose.

The co-operation of the patient is most helpful for progress to be recorded. We advise that the sufferer should patiently sustain the effort for movement, gently and without mental vigour, seeking the coming of new movement, even when it is not there. The reason we advise this is to encourage the nerves to carry the message from the consciousness through the weakened nerve cells to act on the muscles, and thus activate them into performance. When no result is apparent we still advise the continuance of the effort to express the intention through the bodily intelligence for the coming of the objective. It is not necessary to cite examples, for it is a common experience with healing gradually to see function return with many patients. Another good result which takes place concurrently with this is that where muscular wastage has followed the non-activity of the nerves, we witness the restoration of tissue and the building of muscle formation. This also implies that the glandular control of cell reproduction has been energised. Success largely depends upon the patient making himself an ally to the healing and the constant encouragement of relatives and friends, especially with young people. It is natural that one will take the line of least resistance and put up with paralysing weaknesses, so that it becomes a condition to be endured and accepted, thus forming a permanent habit.

It is a common experience in contact healing to see a noticeable improvement. The patient can again (under the healer's purposeful direction) lift his legs and walk more normally instead of shuffling along, but he immediately drops back into the old habit as soon as he motivates himself. Therefore instruction to the patient becomes almost as great an importance as the healing itself. Every movement has to be a slow and ordered one, with the intention sustained throughout the action. Walking has to be done in slow motion at first. It is only through perseverance that the patient is able to take full advantage of the improvements, until more natural and subconscious control comes.

Bad balance usually accompanies paralysis of the lower limbs. The tendency is for patients to hurry as quickly as they can to get to where they are going, to maintain the balance with tensed movement. This is particularly seen with sufferers from disseminated sclerosis. The healer's task is to overcome this tendency and encourage the patient to seek slow, controlled, and ordered movement throughout every stage of a walking step. The difficulty to maintain balance is largely a matter of mental outlook. The fear of falling has to be mastered, with understanding and comprehending advice. The restoring of balance, of course, gradually and naturally comes with better controlled movements as the nerve functions return. Here again the guides are able to assist by influencing the mind and nerves to build confidence and assurance.

Neuritis is another complaint that yields to healing. The physical cause lies in some form of stress, sometimes local, but more often from some mental tension. Neuralgia is symptomatic of this, and usually accompanies headaches that arise from worry and fear. It is true to say that the quality of "fear," either real or imaginary (and most often it belongs to the latter category), is the cause of much nervous unrest promoting the family of troubles associated with neuritis.

The way of the healing follows the same pattern, that of allaying the cause of the fear and soothing the outlook. Neuritis is often a mild reaction of tensions of a lesser kind and, therefore, healers invariably see the trouble quickly ease away as a more contented outlook comes.

It is a general experience with spirit healing, and particularly so with absent healing, for patients, no matter what the character of disease may be, to become aware of a sense of inner upliftment in the early days following treatment. There is a feeling of lightness and happiness with a realisation of assurance and confidence. This effect is an obvious result arising from the help given by the healing guides to smooth out nervousness and restore serenity to the outlook.

There is a theory that, associated with this effort, the sense of physical well-being is produced through the body intelligence via the known glandular systems and the less known ductless glands. Study of mediumship and healership has led to the belief that there exists a ductless glandular system that is contiguous with the sensory nerves of the body. It has one of its receiving terminals behind the nasal cavity, and links through the consciousness with the pineal gland and the pituitary glandular systems. Its main trunk proceeds along the spinal column, ending in the lumbar region. From there it branches throughout the lower body and lower limbs. It is probably this gland that is receptive to the cosmic forces through characterised breathing and responds also to magnetic healing.

When one "feels on top of the world" the whole body is light and exceedingly active, and there must be a reasoned process to account for it. Conversely, when the body feels heavy and fatigued, and it becomes an effort to attempt anything, there is also a reason for this. The theory is advanced that these conditions react from the state of well-being through cosmic nourishment of this ductless gland. This may well account for the amazement of doctors when they wonder where a patient receiving spiritual healing obtains his "strength," for it does appear logical that this ductless gland is a reactor to psychic or spirit directives. If, therefore, this "psychic gland" is associated with the sensory nerves, we have the process by which a happy condition comes to the body and how neuritis can be removed.

It is quite impossible to restrict the consideration of spirit healing to one process. There are many factors involved, of which we, as yet, know little.

Another important aspect of the healing for mental and nervous diseases comes with dealing with patients who are suffering from "obsessions" and "possessions." Cases of actual "possession," by which is meant that the patient's personality is invaded by that of a spirit entity, invariably of a distressing kind, are less in number than may be thought to be the case. In many instances where a child or person behaves illogically and unreasonably the thought often arises in the minds of the relatives that "he has an evil spirit with him." This is accepted sometimes by doctors and psychiatrists without it necessarily being the case.

Obsession takes many forms; it may be harmless or distressing. Even people deemed to be perfectly normal may be said to be obsessed with certain ideas, missions or projects. It is a matter of degree. When the enthusiasm and persistence of a person to propagate a way of thought is too strong, such as with a religious enthusiast, then it is said the individual is obsessed. Perhaps this is more truly described as a lack of appreciation and perspective.

Nevertheless, in healing practice, numbers of distressing obsessions are overcome. Some of these are claustrophobia, persecution, fears of certain foods and contamination, visions and voices. Such illnesses create mental tortures that are more distressing than physical afflictions, and, at times, are obstinate, even to spirit influence.

I recall a young girl who had the contamination complex. Even when she touched the handle of a door she would feel she was filthy and could not rest until she had scrubbed her hands for a long time. This unfortunate girl spent most of her waking life in bathing and washing her hands. She could not follow any ordinary employment or even home service for this reason. She had been taken to nerve specialists and psychiatrists in number. Each had used powers of persuasive reasoning with her, as, of course, her parents had always done, but without avail. She was put to sleep for three weeks, hoping the obsession would die away. She was subjected to hypnosis to lead her mind to renounce the weakness—all without success. Absent healing was sought by the mother. It was reported that following this she became dull in her perception and appreciation for a number of days. She only wanted to sleep.

Then one morning she came down to breakfast looking like a new person. Her eyes were bright and she had the smile that had been lacking for so long. Her parents looked at her in amazement, but wisely made no comment. After she had finished her breakfast they waited for her inevitable going to her room to wash her hands, but she did not do so. Instead, she proceeded to collect the soiled dishes and to *wash them up*, a hitherto undreamt of thing. The change was complete. I kept in touch with the mother for some time, to see whether there was any return of the trouble, but there was not. The specialist in neurotic diseases, who had been consulted several times, declared he had never seen such a change take place in all his experience. It was noted that the daughter became more attached to her father than her mother. When, later on, the wife told her husband and daughter of her seeking spiritual healing and how the good change took place so soon after, both of them pooh-poohed the idea of spiritual help.

When a person is obsessed by remorse for some wrong action in the past, the healing, at times, seems longer delayed than that with seemingly more difficult inner-mind conditions. The reason for this may well be that the physical mind and memory have been so deeply impressed that they remain obstinate. So it is when a patient's mind has been deeply wounded in a love affair, or by the passing of a very near and dear one. This may indicate that the ever-present physical mind upset is more slow to respond to spirit influence from the spirit self than when the disharmony lies in the spirit mind.

In cases of possession, or schizophrenia, or double personality, it often develops into dementia and violence, needing specially qualified healers to treat these cases personally. If the adverse influence is a weak one, then there is a reasonable chance of turning the invading personality away. When the hold on the patient has become strong, healers do not have much opportunity of treating them in person, as usually they are committed to mental hospitals. The contact healing method is done by reasoning with the invading entity, generally by a spirit guide who speaks through an entranced medium. When success follows absent healing, then it is logical to assume that the guides reason with and influence the entity on the spirit side of life to leave the patient alone.

A measure of success is also seen with overcoming mild conditions of insanity. If the patient is at home, then this more easily takes place, but there are numbers of cases on record where patients in mental institutions recover balance and perspective and are able to return to their families cured. These results usually take place through absent healing. As the patient recovers, he or she is at first allowed home on parole for a short time, and then for longer periods, until there is no need to return for restraining hospital treatment.

A statement has been made in the past that Spiritualism induces insanity. There is no evidence to support it. Indeed in the reports of the Lunacy Commissioners there has not been one case of insanity directly attributable to this cause. On the other hand, appreciable numbers of afflicted people have been successfully treated through spiritual healing. What is also important, though unprovable, many more have been prevented from degenerating into lunacy through the corrective influence received from a spirit guide.

Thus the healing picture for mental and nervous diseases shows a dual pattern. The first is the removal on the thought plane of the causes of stress within the total self of the patient.

Secondly, the soothing of physical and nervous tensions and the stimulation of co-ordination and control of the sensory and motor nerves.

Here is a field of healing that is as yet little appreciated by medical authorities. While they admit that the state of mind plays so large a part in physical well-being, only scant attention in advanced medical practice is paid to the study and investigation of mind conditions. The reason may be that the mind cannot be placed under a microscope, and physical science is too limited in its scope to ascertain the laws that govern this essential part of the person.

For the last fifteen years the author, with Mr. and Mrs. Burton, has sat regularly once a week for instruction and guidance in the whole realm of spirit healing. The guide in control of the spirit healing organisation speaks through the author in trance, and a number of his instructions have been preserved on tape recordings. In this way, much knowledge has been gained, especially with the cause and treatment of mind conditions. When medical practitioners are willing to co-operate with healership they too will add to their understanding through receiving instruction and knowledge by listening to their spirit contemporaries.

The extent to which it may be assessed that healing of nerve \ and other diseases has taken place is variable. Judgment may vary according to the attitude of mind of the observer. At times judgment is reached by a consideration of the state of a patient after healing without due regard to all the circumstances. For example, a sufferer from paralysis who has lost the total use of his legs is, according to doctors, past any effective treatment. When, with spirit healing, co-ordination and control gradually return to the useless legs, the patient is able again to stand erect and to walk with the aid of a stick, and he is pointed out as being an example of spirit healing, the observer, noticing the need for a stick and possibly some hesitation in correct leg movements, may be inclined to the opinion that the healing has failed. There have been cases where a spinal curvature has been largely corrected, and yet a bone-growth deformity of the shoulder is still noticeable. Through the years this deformity had developed consequent on the curvature. Because it is not possible for the healing to remove the excessive | bone mass, it is concluded that the healing has been non-successful. Incidentally, there are cases on record, and particularly with younger people, where such deformities have gradually diminished | with the continuance of the healing directive.

I recall a young lad, about twelve years of age, who was carried by a healer on to the platform at the Victoria Hall in London. He had to be carried, for he had suffered from birth from a nervous disease that prevented his sitting upright, or to have any use in his legs. He was medically regarded as a completely hopeless case. The doctors said he could never walk. On this occasion, his spine was partially straightened and he could sit more upright and hold up his head. There was no apparent benefit to his legs. The healer carried him away. In the months that followed, he continued to seek the coming of co-ordination through contact healing, week by week. I was kept informed of the boy's condition and we included him in our absent healing intercessions.

Slowly life began to come to the hitherto useless legs. After a while he was given crutches to help him hobble about. As the healing continued, he was able to discard these aids. The healer patiently maintained his treatment for the patient over the years. It was his reward to see the progressive improvement, until the lad approached manhood and was able to go to work and live a fairly normal life.

Ten years after he was carried, quite helpless, into the Victoria Hall, he was able to walk down the aisle of a church in Surrey with his bride on his arm. The only sign of his previous trouble was a slight roll of the hips. When a friend was told that the bridegroom had been receiving spiritual healing, the reply came: "Well, it's not done him much good; he cannot walk straight."

The author has also known doctors, who observing the presence of some physical defect, use it as an excuse to avoid recognition of the benefit that healing has brought for the previous serious troubles that were medically incurable. After all, assessment of healing is a matter of fair judgment.

CHAPTER FIFTEEN

SUPERNORMAL HEALINGS

This book is being written in the spring, and the cherry trees are in bloom. In order to show the diversity of successful healings, I am dipping into my "Special Files" for the first three months of this year. These special files are the only ones that can be kept. With a postbag of over 10,000 letters a week it is quite impossible to keep individual case records. It would need the employment of many filing clerks and extensive floor space for the files. On an average over a thousand new applications for spiritual healing are received every week. Many of them are soon healed. Thus there is an ever-changing category of patients that would render the keeping of detailed records a useless procedure. Apart from what may be described as "normal" healing results, there are those where the disease is considered "incurable." When these are healed they are filed under their disease headings. For such diseases as leukemia, we keep all the letters pertaining to them, but otherwise the mass of letters are burnt after they have been answered and intercession given. The reason why they are burnt is that many letters contain intimate and personal details. Naturally all letters are confidential. No reference is ever made to them, unless permission has been given. Therefore in the citations that follow, which are extracts from the actual letters received, no names or any indication who the writer may be are given.

All these "Special File" letters are kept in case the references are challenged by any *bona-fide* person or organisation, so that we can prove their authenticity.

Over the years we have been at the Sanctuary at Shere, there have amassed records of over 30,000 of these outstanding super-normal spirit healings, which cover almost every disease and ill-condition that afflicts humanity. It may be noted that this is the result of the efforts of only one healing band. When it is remembered that there are now a great number of healing groups associated with Spiritualist churches, and thousands of healers who voluntarily give their time to heal the sick, the grand total of people who have received benefit must be enormous. This success everywhere has built, day by day, the public support for spiritual healing.

After I took part in a B.B.C. television programme, where the odds were heavily against me, the B.B.C. received more letters (mainly protesting) than they had received with any previous feature. This led the B.B.C. to take the unprecedented action of conducting a national audience survey on spiritual healing. I was told by an important B.B.C. official that these surveys cost thousands of pounds, and therefore they are ordered only for exceptional reasons. The findings of this survey has been kept a very close secret by the B.B.C., but from a high authority I was told that over ninety per cent. of the people interrogated believed in spiritual healing and that over sixty per cent. supported the healing methods as conducted by myself, my collaborators and other Spiritualist healers.

Such general public support has developed upon success and not upon non-success. In some efforts to depreciate spiritual healing, doctors and others have pointed to cases where no result has occurred. We freely admit that there are cases that do not respond as we would wish, and a chapter has been devoted to this. It is suggested that the proof of healing does not rest on this small minority but on the benefits conferred on the great majority of the sick who have been helped to recover. The limited selection of the reports that follow give a general indication of this act.

3.1.59
"Mr. 'W.' was said to be suffering from an advanced state of cancer. When he went into hospital for an operation a snippet was

taken from his bowel and sent to the pathologist for testing. Two days later the surgeon visited his bedside with the pathologist's report. He said that an extraordinary thing had happened, and there was now no need for an operation for there is no trace of cancer, and he would see him in six months time. He also made the comment: 'I have not seen such a thing happen for eight years'."

17.1.59.

"I am the parson you were good enough to treat for my weak hearing in my right ear and for stone deafness in my left one. The left ear has so remarkably improved that the right ear now feels the stuffier and my hearing is so much better. Indeed I have the impression that people are shouting. I did not mention it to you, not wishing to appear too much of a hypochondriac, but for some three months past, I have had a very painful rheumatism in each shoulder. On rising this morning (the day following your treatment) there are no aches in the right shoulder and much lesser ones in the left. Coincidence or not, it makes me wonder."

20.1.59.

(Canada.) "My son-in-law was taken to hospital dying from cardiac thrombosis. An eminent heart specialist was sent for from Minnesota. He prepared my daughter for the worst, for there was 'no hope'. When she left him he was delirious and sinking. I cabled for your help ... and when the specialist again visited him, he said a change has taken place. It is a miracle; by all standards he should have died, twice over. He is now well, and back at home."

25.1.59.

"Eight days have passed since I brought my baby to you (*Note*: she was blind). The improvement in her eyes is tremendous. She can now see quite small items some distance away and the once continuous movement of the eyes hardly exist at all. I really knew that once I had brought her to you for spiritual healing all would be well, but expected it to take months before any noticeable improvement was observed. I never thought it would come so quickly."

27.1.59.

"Some four or five years ago my father asked your help for my brother who was desperately ill with Hodgkinson's Disease. Now he is thought by the doctors to be a 'living miracle', having fully recovered."

29.1.59.
"Seven years ago you treated my husband. He had the severest injuries, including a fractured skull, contusion of the brain, a fractured femur, etc. I was told at the hospital that there was very little hope that he would recover, but thanks to you, he has, and is now living a full and happy life with only one minor disability."

30.1.59.
"Here is the record. J.C., aged 58—Hospital, Belfast. January 13, coronary thrombosis. January 14 to 18, very ill and weakening. January 20, wife told by specialist, 'No hope at all'. Son sent for and I telephoned you for help. January 21, patient had a better night. Son saw specialist, who said that since telling wife there was ho hope, the heart had suddenly improved and there was now hope. Patient reading the paper. January 22, good night. Patient cheerful and eating. Son (in Navy) told he could return to his unit overseas. Since then he has continued to maintain progress. My wife and I are convinced that some power outside the medical world has saved him."

2.2.59.
"I must write again and tell you how much better I am. My hips and knees are really wonderful (that is the only expression I can use). Just a little stiff sometimes but apart from that 'nothing.' I look back before your healing started when I was in such pain, and I cannot believe it is myself now. Also I even find myself singing and whistling, which I haven't done for years."

4.2.59.
"I am writing for my brother, he was in the University College Hospital, London. His gullet had closed up, no food could pass through it. He had to be fed through a tube. Your letter could not have come at a better time, for he was so very weak, but he was greatly pleased to get it. My next piece of news may seem fantastic, but yesterday morning he ate egg and bacon through his gullet just like any other person, and when I tell you he has not eaten anything like that for a month, you can imagine how much he enjoyed it. He puts this down to your help, for there can be no other reason."

5.2.59.

"You may remember I visited you in the early Spring of 1955. I was suffering from a stone in the ureter. You told me that you hoped the stone would be disintegrated. The day before I saw you the X-ray showed the stone very clearly, but when the surgeon operated some few days afterwards, she could not find it. She thought it must have broken up into sediment, for there were traces of this in the catheter, two days later. The next X-ray showed nothing and it has not troubled me since."

14.2.59.

"I feel that I ought to write to you in connection with the absent healing that you gave me last year. As far back as since last August there has been no recurrence of the persistent head noises and the subsequent deafness from which I had previously suffered. At first I was a bit dubious about the whole thing, but having this treatment from you my complete outlook on the whole thing is changed."

18.2.59.

"After seeing you that day she has not looked back, so far as her walking is concerned. As you know, at the same time that you treated her arthritis you also treated her for gall stones for which she was entering hospital on the following day to have them surgically removed. You asked that we insisted upon new X-ray plates being taken before any operation was performed. She was in hospital for a few days for another condition, and when this was cleared up it was decided to take further X-ray plates, to see afresh the gall stone position. Eight plates were taken and it was discovered she had none at all; they had all vanished."

21.2.59.

"Almost two years ago I witnessed a demonstration of healing by you in Glasgow. As a general practitioner I examined a patient before and after healing and was truly amazed at what had happened. It was an experience which I shall never forget. I am now seeking your help for my own state of health."

27.2.59.

"I am ever so much better since I saw you last Thursday. I shall never forget it. You took from me the sentence of death, or much worse, disablement for life. I am able to get out of the bath and to stand on a chair and get the family meals, none of which I was able to do before. And the lump in my neck has practically disappeared."

16.3.59.

"I am a teacher of dancing ... When we were having a lesson this weekend with H.K. he told me of the wonderful cure you effected on his knee ... It is quite miraculous to see him dance on that leg. All the doctors said he would not dance again, but after writing to you he was demonstrating again in a month."

18.3.59.

"A week has elapsed since you painlessly adjusted the misplaced vertebrae at the base of my neck ... Not only am I able to enjoy once again the freedom of head movement but also my whole body has undergone a complete change. The left arm which I had previously avoided using as much as possible to prevent pain is now loose and completely free and co-ordinated. My shoulders no longer ache and the continuous pain in my left collar bone is now a forgotten memory; also the extreme pain on the left side of my neck has practically gone. At no time during the week have I had the slightest suggestion of a recurrence of the stiffness, not even on rising in the morning. The whole action of my spine is free, extending even to my hip joints, giving my whole body rhythmic suppleness and co-ordination."

20.3.59.

"I am most anxious to give you the good news concerning my sister. She is almost fit enough to leave the mental hospital and has put on a stone in weight. The psychiatrist himself cannot understand such a swift recovery. He went on to explain that it took five of the staff to attend to her when she was aggressive. But now after the healing she is cheering up the other patients, and in three weeks time we shall have her home. My son too, has recovered from his glandular trouble."

6.4.59.

"It is long past the time to report to you on the condition of my daughter's hands. I apologise for this though it was deliberate on my part. There has been a startling improvement in the skin complaint. So decided was the change that I thought it could not possibly be maintained, but it has, thanks to you. Her hands have kept the improvement so much that they are really beautiful—new skin, smooth and with a fresh healthy pink colour."

The following letters refer to another aspect of healing:

25.2.59.
"I am very pleased to tell you of the great help you brought to me when I was having my baby. I was delivered of a lovely baby girl without any trouble at all. I explained to you before how I was held when I had my last two children. Well, in comparison, I did not know I was going to have this baby. I had a much quicker labour and no hospital either. I made such good progress every time I was examined, so the nurse and doctor knew I would be able to deliver this baby at home, which I did without any chloroform or forceps, in fact I didn't even have to have any stitches ..."

Undated.
"I am writing to say 'thank you' for all your help. After thirteen years of waiting we have a beautiful baby girl, and through the whole labour I was quietly comforted by the thoughts of help and strength that reached me."

6.3.59.
"We are very proud to have this baby after being told it was impossible to have one."

It will be noted that numbers of the reports refer to healings that have taken place in the past, the reason being that they were used in an introductory way before seeking healing for someone else. These are specially included in the selection in order to provide evidence of the permanence of healing. About three thousand letters of this character are received every year. In addition there are, of course, the thousands of other reports testifying to improvement and recoveries. It is estimated these number half a million annually.

The last three letters mention help given in childbirth and for the coming of a baby. Regarding the latter, it is presumed this healing assistance is given when there exists a physical weakness with one or both of the partners. Through the healing this weakness is overcome thus opening the way for children to be conceived.

I recall the case of a mother whose first baby caused so much trouble that it imperilled her life and the baby was lost. The mother was strongly advised not to have further babies. As time went on another baby was on its way. Special precautions were made to deal with the event. At a Kingston hospital it was arranged that an eminent gynæcologist from a London hospital would specially come as soon as the birth became imminent. Spiritual healing was sought from the first days following conception. With the early signs of labour the mother was admitted to the hospital and a telephone call made to the specialist. The woman was asked to wait for a short while. She sat in the waiting room with her mother. While she was waiting the baby came naturally—in the waiting-room!

Another case was that of a woman who was having her first baby at thirty-nine years of age, and some natural apprehension was felt. Our healing was sought for her. During the labour she went to the commode, and before she could get back the little one arrived, without any fuss or stress.

All my daughters have given me grandchildren, and in each case the birth was exceptionally easy. On one occasion the baby arrived without any labour pains and my daughter, of course, knew of the fact and called the nurse. When she was told, she pooh-poohed the idea, and proceeded to tuck my daughter up in bed. It was only with difficulty that the nurse was induced to look and see—and behold, the baby had been born.

The General Medical Council would doubtless be surprised to know that in the first three months of this year I have received eighty-two letters from the members of the British Medical Association. Of course, all these letters are received under the seal of confidence. I will quote some sentences from these doctors' letters:

"My wife asks me to say there is a continued improvement, that I can confirm."

"My family are all now very well. With 'X' the symptoms of high blood pressure have abated. With 'Y' there is marked improvement in the headaches and the dizziness."

"My wife has now fully recovered. 'A' is in good health, and cheerful, being able to spend a lot of time in the garden."

"Since communicating with you I have found that I am tiring less and capable of greater physical effort."

"My catarrh continues to remain much improved. My general health also gives me greater confidence with a definite improvement of my nervous system."

"From the evidence I have already been privileged to receive I look forward in this coming year to further improvement in my ear condition. May I also say that my association with you has also made a tremendous difference to my outlook on life."

"Again good news. I'm very delighted with this week. My wife has had six good days and only one day of a moderately severe attack."

"A sudden remarkable change has taken place with 'B'. I had your letter in my pocket when I visited him this morning, telling that you had started treatment. I found him sitting up, doing a jig-saw puzzle; his temperature was normal; most puzzling to me, yet he is better, without any reason that I am aware of."

"If I could understand your methods I would be better able to appreciate how the transformation has come to both the patients I asked you to help. When I wrote to you, it was with 'my tongue in my cheek' and because Dr. 'C' had recommended you. . . . The allaying of the painful symptoms was not the result of the medicines in either case, therefore I can only attribute the change for the better from you. . . ."

"Thank you, I am now very much better and can accept a normal diet."

"I am wondering if I have come through the influenza epidemic which has been most severe in this district, without contracting it, is in any way due to you . . . my colleagues have had it. I know that my vitality is better and I can do more each day than I previously could, without being aware of fatigue."

Some of these doctors and others have come to the Sanctuary for personal healing, while others accompany their patients. When I know that a doctor is present, and without referring to his profession, I invite him to check the ill-condition, such as poker-back spines, before treatment begins, so that he can see for himself the state of the patient. Then I allow the doctor's hand to be under mine, as flexibility is restored, or a curvature is straightened, so that he can actually feel the mobility or realignment come. I have always found the doctors ready to admit the beneficial change that has taken place.

Last year a few medical students came to observe the healing and, judging from our conversation afterwards, they were very much impressed. It so happened, a while later, that I received an invitation to speak on spirit healing at their monthly meeting— but at the eleventh hour it was cancelled. Why?

While we witness rapid and sometimes instantaneous healing, the extracts show that the usual way of healing is by a gradual and progressive means, as the following report indicates:—

August 16. " 'A' entered hospital suffering from bulba polio. Immediate operation for trachiotomy, the throat muscles being paralysed. She could not talk or take food. August 18. She was put into an automatic breathing machine. Medical opinion was that 'A' could not live more than three hours. You were contacted at this time for urgent healing by telephone. The doctors said the paralysis which had affected the neck, brain and the top half of the body was closing in on the heart. The beats were becoming fainter and slower. The left lung had stopped operating altogether and her eyes were sunken in a death-like mask. Nine hours later she was still alive and I was just able to recognise her. Her passing was still a foregone conclusion to take place at any time. The doctors and nurses attending her could not understand how it was that she lived through the night and the next day or where she obtained her vital strength from. August 20 to 24. Life was maintained and she appeared to become just a little brighter and there was a little colour in her cheeks. August 26. She began to breath without assistance through the tube in her neck. The sisters say she has amazing will power. Progress was slowly maintained until September 9th when signs of life returned for her voice. Progress continued, words could be formed and this went on until September 20th, when she was able to lift her head from the pillow. Speaking more naturally now. On September 23rd the feeding tube was extracted and 'A' able to take eight ounces of fluid. The doctors still cannot understand why she is improving, they say it is not due to their efforts. Progress continued and by October 6th she is getting on 'like a house on fire.' She sat up for one and a half hours and has been trying to walk. On November 3rd, 'A' was able to walk all round the room. Steady progress continues. She can eat the inside of toast now and has put on eight pounds. November 26. 'A' left the hospital for convalescence but has to attend the hospital for physiotherapy three times a week. One year later; It would now be hard to tell that she ever suffered from polio."

It will be noted that absent healing commenced when 'A' was hourly expected to die. With the help received by letter this was constantly maintained. The doctors recognised there was something additional to the good help they gave her that maintained her through the critical days. The healing lasted three months.

Distance presents no obstacle to absent healing and reports of supernormal healings come from the other side of the world. An example of this is the story that follows, written by Lady Baden-Powell, who herself has been successfully treated for arthritis and other troubles. It was in the early part of 1959 that she was involved in an accident, breaking some ribs. She particularly wished to travel to fulfil an important engagement in connection with the Girl Guide movement and she wrote asking for urgent help to enable her to carry it out. This she did, and when the strapping around her chest was taken off it was found the ribs had healed fully. Lady Baden-Powell wrote the following letter while she was touring South Africa carrying on the Scout tradition inaugurated by her husband. It reads: —

"The warmest and most intense admiration comes to you in fullest measure for what you have achieved, so wonderfully, for my niece. She has been fearfully ill with a damaged back, doctors had operated on her, and she was getting worse and worse. One specialist said that she would never get right and would be invalided for the rest of her life.

"You will know what that means to a young, vigorous, fine young woman in her thirties, married to a farmer, just embarking on making their new life together, and starting their farm with little money and the necessity for being well.

"Through her friend (Mr. 'X' of Hove) she got into touch with you and what you have done is indeed the most amazing miracle that anybody could imagine. She is not only well, but is in the saddle on her wild 2,000-acre farm, riding up the steep mountain sides, hour after hour, herding her cattle, seeing to the fencing of this virgin land; overseeing the dipping of her 500 sheep; coping with the making of the farm homestead and above that acting as the local J.P. for the Africans, secretary to the Farmers' Union, wise and active counsellor to the East Africa Women's League and being a generous hostess to all and sundry.

"Thanks to you, she is strong, fit and happy— and even to her intense pleasure, being a great horsewoman, breeding, training, and riding and winning a race or two in the local gymkhanas."

Here is another story from far afield. The writer is a judge's wife in Oklahoma, U.S.A.:

"Here is the report you asked for. My husband was involved in an automobile smash. As a result of this and following operations to his neck and back, he became totally paralysed from his waist downwards, which also lost for him control over his bowels. He spent his days either in bed or in a wheeled chair. His great tragedy was that he could no longer attend the courts or take any active interest in life any more. It was on the advice of our pastor that I wrote to you, not really thinking you could do anything for him, after all our professors had given us the information that nothing in their ability could do anything to restore him.

"I got your first letter in July last year, and hoping against hope that you might be able to help him, I continued to send you letters regularly. My husband read your letters of hope and he used to look forward to them eagerly. Three weeks after your first letter he just stood up one day and walked along the veranda to his and our great joy. From this day, his strength returned and his movements improved. Control came for his bowel actions. By the end of August he was able to walk some distance with the aid of a strong stick. The nobbly projection in his spine, where the surgeons said it had been broken and which made him bend over double, went back into its place. In October he was able to resume his court work.

"It is now seven months since I first wrote to you, and I cannot see any signs of weakness and he never complains of anything. It is, I think, time for you now to leave off your treatment, for he is so well.

"You will be interested, I think, to know that his doctor friends look at him and just shake their heads, for they cannot believe what they see. My husband never tires in singing praises of you. When he tells his friends the hospital doctors where he first was taken, about your healing, they cannot deny what he says, but they go on shaking their heads, for they just cannot understand it. Our debt of gratitude can never be repaid in any form. . ."

Many, many more stories of healing could be included, but those already given should be enough to provide the full answer to the sceptic, and to justify our claim that through the power of the Spirit that which is impossible to medical science becomes a reality through spiritual healing. Lastly, it should be borne in mind that whereas the testimonies given in this chapter are in the realm of the supernormal, there are a multitude of other healings of less serious conditions. Any *bona-fide* investigator can, by arrangement, come and scan through any post. He can watch the letters come in (sealed), and open and read them (in confidence) to see that our claims can be proved to the hilt.

There is, however, one more story, of particular interest, insofar as it concerns a child thought to be totally incurable. The following extracts are taken from the newspaper that reviewed the healing over a year later:

"They say that this bonny little girl, with fair curly hair, who dances, skips and runs like all the other children at West Street Nursery School, Colne, is a miracle.

"A miracle. For Barbara was born a spastic, she was blind, mentally and physically retarded. She was twice, as a baby, given up for lost, as she lay gravely ill from pneumonia, and even though she recovered from the pneumonia, she remained a spastic and medical opinion said she was doomed to a life of being pitied.

"Her mother carried Barbara on to the stage at Colne's Municipal Hall when Mr. Edwards gave a demonstration of spirit healing. Barbara was then two and a half years old. She could not walk. She had difficulty in even raising her head. Mr. Edwards, our reporter remembers, smiled at the little girl in the green dress. He asked her mother to put Barbara down. He then took Barbara's hands in his own and asked her to walk. The audience gasped as Barbara, who had never walked before, took her first few uncertain paces forward.

"Six months later, Barbara was walking properly and is now almost a normal child ... And says Barbara's headmistress: 'I didn't use to believe in spiritual healing, but I do now. I think Barbara is marvellous!'"

The local vicar, the Rev. Geoffrey Petts, in commenting on this case said: "Barbara is just one of many thousands who have received permanent benefit from spirit healing. Barbara's healing, like that of others, was not a miracle, for a miracle is an event due to some supernatural agency, whereas there is nothing supernatural in spirit healing. On the contrary is very much a natural phenomenon.

"Science is revealing daily that a materialistic view of life is no longer tenable. It is not more feasible to suppose that man can be accounted for entirely in terms of biology, psychology, etc., than it is to suppose that matter is solid, which—as everyone must surely know in these days of atomic structures, weights, energies— is not so.

"The evidence points to the belief that man has a spiritual as well as a material nature. He is more than flesh and blood that ends in the grave. The evidence points to the existence of agencies or forces beyond those capable of being measured by instruments. This evidence is helping to support the claim of the spirit healer; that man is a being possessing a spirit which affects and is affected by the body; that illness is bound up with an unbalance between the two natures, material and spiritual; that he, the healer, is the instrument of a force or power which is present in the universe and which, when brought to bear on disorder, disharmony, helps to, if not completely, restore order and harmony.

"This healing is not new in the sense that it is a phenomenon of our time. The 'miracles' of Jesus were none other than a manifestion of this same power, which has always been present, but which has not been recognised or understood save in part until now. It is in no sense supernatural. It does not depend on the knowledge of the sufferers to be healed. It does not depend on religous faith or any other kind of faith. Spirit healing is not faith healing. It is a power that works in its own right and those who have taken the trouble to understand, see it and use it as a normal part of life.

"Mr. Edwards is probably the greatest spirit healer of our time, but he is not alone in his ministry. Every area has its one or two who quietly seek to relieve the sick of their misfortune.

"As is to be expected, many will find it hard to accept these facts, none more so than the medical fraternity. One can sympathise with their position, but let it be said in all charity that outright condemnation of spirit healing is sheer foolishness and savours of prejudice.

"Contrary to some ideas, spirit healing neither seeks to decry nor displace orthodox medicine. Its wish is that the two should work together. Spirit healers recognise the function and the great value of orthodox medicine and all they ask is that their work should be given the consideration that it warrants."

With what clearer thoughts can this chapter on testimony be ended?

CHAPTER SIXTEEN

GENERAL CONCLUSIONS

The question may be asked: "Why is it that, when doctors and others go into a wider realm of activity on entering spirit life, they should bother themselves by seeking additional knowledge so that they can help those whom they have left behind on earth?" It may be thought that with all the opportunities of enjoying the new way of life, with its higher perception and appreciation of the arts and philosophies, why should they be willing to limit their efforts by continuing to heal the earthly sick through healership?

The answer may be found in two directives. The first is that there is a much higher purpose in healing than curing, say Mr. Smith of London of his arthritis. In the full scheme of things this may not appear of very great importance, though of course, it is vitally important to Mr. Smith and his family. *There must be some greater purpose.*

From the earliest days in the history of mankind there has always existed an inner urge to do something more and to be discontented with the prevailing way of life. Any animal given protection from the weather, a mate and food, is quite contented and does not seek anything further. Give a man similar advantages and he is not contented with them but seeks further achievement. In reviewing the history of mankind we find another common link. No matter whether people belong to an advanced civilisation or whether they are primitive savages, they all, with few exceptions worship and fear a God. Their conceptions of a God and the after-life reflect the aspirations and outlook of the time. Further, as man progressed, and enjoyed the privilege of possessing things, so there

arose an inner desire to preserve those possessions by living at
peace with his neighbours.

These qualities that mankind has always possessed, and still
does, indicate the presence of a non-physical, mental idealism that
is not related to gross earthy concerns. It is this that denotes the
presence of the soul of man, or, as we term it, his spirit self.

We see in the laws that govern our creation the purpose of
spiritual progression. It is more than cold evolution, for that is
but the result of physical cause and effect.

Human progression has ever sought for a higher way of life
based upon spiritual satisfaction. Yet no progress can be achieved
in advance of man's appreciation of the values of life.

The coming of Jesus at a critical time in the history of mankind
gave the spiritual directives for our right living and demonstrated
the power of the Spirit in healing the sick. The growth of the Early
Church has been attributed by historians to the dual practice of
preaching the new truths and healing the sick. With this growth
also came the desire for personal power and possession of wealth
by the Church and the gift of healing gradually faded away.

It may well be that, in these days, with the advancement of
scientific knowledge, plus the coming of another critical time in
the history of man, where material concerns tend to overwhelm
spiritual thought, that the gift of healing has been resurrected to
demonstrate the truth of man's spirituality and brotherhood.
People to-day are hungry for spiritual direction that they can
accept in reason. This has been shown with the vast audiences
that gather to listen to evangelists, as they did when Billy Graham
came here. Unfortunately, it is admitted that this endeavour to
provide an impetus for people to return to church worship has
failed—and the Church must accept the responsibility for this—
for the people were willing.

People to-day, and especially the younger generation, are not
content to accept legendary ritual and archaic theologies, on the
basis of blind faith and belief. They require something that is
tangible. It is through spiritual healing that the proof of the soul
and spirit is given. With the evidence of individual survival after

this phase of life has passed a new spiritual concept of life can arise.

I again refer to the B.B.C. national audience survey, when I was informed that over ninety per cent. accepted spiritual healing. The spiritual fire continues with us, though it may be damped down and smouldering. It can never die out, for it is inherent within us. It only needs the application of reasoned proof to re-awaken the embers into flame again. The time for belief in the power of the priest alone has gone. The sooner the Church as a whole realises this the better. When the Church substitutes for the "power of the priest" the "power of the Spirit" that can be demonstrated through them, and the sick are healed in public services before the altar, so will people receive that spiritual food for which they are hungry. The Church will then regain its place in the divine plan, to guide man's destines.

It may be we are witnessing to-day the unfolding of a Plan to influence our lives by new activity through spiritual healing in which the spirit doctors are playing their part as missionaries for the future. Just as we have, in the past, sent missionaries with special qualifications to heal the sick, to help backward peoples, so it may be, in a much larger sense, there exists this greater purpose behind present-day healing successes.

Sure advancement in the scientific as well as the spiritual realm can only be of gradual yet progressive growth, but this is dependent upon a full appreciation of all the contributory factors. Realisation follows such appreciation. As the news spreads that those who are sick, especially the "incurables," are made well by spiritual means, so they will realise that they must be part spirit now in order to be able to receive from Spirit. As this knowledge spreads and overcomes the prejudices of the vested interests of both Church and Medicine, so mankind as a whole will be led to seek a change in the material code of values that animates the purposes of life to-day.

Thus we can begin to see the greater purpose that is behind the healing of the sick by spirit means, to widen man's outlook, and to spiritualise his way of life, outlawing war, poverty, greed and all other ignoble things.

We are witnessing the unfolding of the divine plan of ordered and conscious progression which in the end will be far more durable than, say, any sudden miraculous transformation in our way of living.

In the early years of the past century the means of establishing communication between spirit and earthly life was of a much cruder form. Mediumship developed more on the lines of manifestations of a physical kind, designed to impress the human intelligence of its supernormal character. This form of mediumship has gradually changed as the implications have been observed. The next step was seen in the progress of mental mediumship, as with clairvoyance and trance control, to give us proof of individual survival and advanced teachings to show us the greater purpose that underlies our physical existence and open our vision to the limitless progression in spirit life that lies before each of us. These latter gifts of the Spirit will not die away, for their purpose can never be fully achieved. The third milestone in the march of understanding is now seen in the growth of healership, coming at the right time, when the burden of sickness is so pressing, as it is in these days.

If a savant of a century ago, living in a time when epidemics wiped out so many people, before the days of antiseptics and medical hygiene, could have visualised the tremendous advances that medical science has made, he would surely have been justified in expecting to see a fully healthy community. The hospitals would be empty, except for emergency cases, and doctors would have little to do. Instead of this happier state of affairs, our hospitals are full to overflowing and those waiting for admission for treatment are numbered by the hundreds of thousands. Doubtless many are dying because there are not the full facilities to treat everyone who is in need. Our doctors are overworked, and an all-embracing national system for the treatment of the sick has had to be instituted by Acts of Parliament. The diseases of cancer and poliomyelitis present scourges that have been increasing with the years. The diseases that have followed nervous stress have increased to alarming proportions. Thus humanity is to-day in a greater need than ever before. So it may well be thought that the coming of spiritual healing is of divine intention, to help the human family in its need and to show the true way of life for the future.

At the present time, our attention is largely focused upon the purpose of spiritual healing to overcome the causes and symptoms of stress after they have been created. We have cause to marvel at the manner in which our ill-conditions are overcome, and there is much exercising of thought as to the way of their performance. Yet it may be that there remains a still greater function for spiritual healing than curing disease, and that is the *prevention of disease*.

Let us again look at cancer. Is its cause physical or spiritual? For half a century the best brains in the medical world have been constantly devoted to finding out its cause from a physical origin. It is pertinent to ask, "Why have they failed?" May it not be, therefore, that the cause is not physical at all? We have pointed out, following the advice given from the spirit guides and our understanding of the condition, that the origin of cancer is a spiritual one. Its causation arises from deep emotional frustrations that are contrary to the natural and free expression of life's purpose. We are witnessing, at present, the slow acceptance of this thesis by eminent medical men. In the U.S.A. and Canada research is being conducted on these lines. Even when it is proved by statistics, and from the intimate study of the character and inner feelings of those who have become cancerous, that the primary causation originates in this field, it appears that physical science will not be able to prevent or overcome it, for it lies quite outside its province.

What, then, is left? This can only be spiritual healing, for it is proved that within its jurisdiction can come the treatment and influence of the mind and spirit self. If it is admitted that such good influence does exist, and it has been the purpose of this book to prove that it does, the prevention of cancer is available. It is a matter of appreciating the spirit potential and seek its aid in preventing the disease coming by administering correct directives to overcome the frustrations.

The application of this is seen by recalling the first general impressions that accompany the beginning of healing, the patients become conscious of inner strength, a feeling of well-being and inner upliftment.

As a rule, Spiritualists and others who accept the truth of conscious survival after death and reunion with loved ones, have no fear of death. The bereaved are comforted by knowing that their dear ones have simply progressed into a new and happier way of life that one day they, too, will enter. By this means there is removed that primal fear and emotional grief that may well contain the beginnings for the origin of cancer. As this knowledge of survival, with its philosophical implications, is accepted by more and more people, this aspect of mind torture will be removed. No more will religions preach about the terrors of hell-fire, and the agonies of purgatory, which do not literally exist. Religion will take on a higher purpose, and awaken mankind generally to the acknowledgment of the spirit heritage that lies before us all, and from which none can escape. The fundamental outlook on life will change into a happier one.

As the implications of spirit healing become more generally accepted and intimately understood, it will become part of our natural home life. Its benefit will be sought as freely as to-day we apply other home remedies to heal minor troubles. This will imply an acceptance of spiritual values and knowledge of our personal intimacy with Spirit as well as the spirit faculty within our make-up.

It can be visualised that there will come an advance in the education of the people on a spiritual level. Physical life will receive its truer perspective in relation to the total life. With this there must come a considerable lessening in the primal fears based on the importance of earthly existence. Mankind will then view this life as an apprenticeship for the greater life.

Thus spiritual healers have not only the task of healing the body but also the soul, by advancing teachings that healing and survival imply.

We shall probably see another advance in the purpose of mediumship and healership, with spirit teachings to show the means to reach the new way of life.

Until this change comes over man's mental horizons (and this may take a decade or two) the work of preventing cancer must necessarily be limited to the activities of healers treating people individually. As the cause of cancer becomes more common knowledge, those who are conscious of inner unhappinesses and frustrations will go to the healer to seek redress and easement far more than they do at present. This in itself will imply the sufferer has the knowledge of the danger of inner-self disharmony, a sure step on the road to spiritual awareness, and by so doing he or she will avoid the coming of cancer.

To-day more and more people of good will and spiritual intent are seeking the development of their healing gift. The number of practising healers of, say, ten years ago, has multiplied several times over. At the time of writing the number is estimated to be in the region of five thousand in the United Kingdom. The demand is insistent for more healers to cope with the great mass of physical and mental sickness in the country to-day. The same story is also being told in other countries. Pioneering work is proceeding in France, Holland and Switzerland and in parts of the U.S.A. where the law proscribes spiritual healing. But no truth can ever be smothered for long.

With the coming of more healers there will also arise the need for a fuller recognition of the ultimate purpose behind the divine spirit plan. The education of both healers and the public will progressively assume increased importance.

To support the ultimate purpose that lies behind spiritual healing comes this need to educate ourselves to all its implications. The way in which the spirit guides will assist us in coming to this wider understanding is illustrated from some extracts from the advice given by the universally loved guide, Silver Birch, to the author some time ago. These indicate the pattern of things to come and support the conclusions put forward. The guide said: "Keep your eyes on the one purpose, and that is to awaken souls to the reality of life. That is the reason, the main reason, for all spirit activity. Nothing else matters. The healing, and the comfort that is attained, draw attention to the message that all who live are part of the

Great Spirit, are spiritual beings, who must realise that so that they shall claim their heritage and fulfil their destiny.

"If all the great heights to which humanity can ascend were easy of attainment, they would not be worth while. The soul finds itself, not through ease, not through leisure, not through idleness, but through toil and striving and difficulty. Those of you who perform your acts of healing, and think how easy all this is, are only looking at the surface. They forget that behind it all there are the years of struggle before the present pinnacle has been reached. You must realise that every peak when it is reached reveals another peak that has to be scaled as well.

"You who belong to the world of matter and have to face the daily problems and obstacles of your material bodies, sometimes become so engrossed with these purely material things that you lose sight of the great spiritual realities behind them.

"We are confronted again and again with the human element in your world and ours. The law is perfect but it has to work through imperfect beings. What you cannot control is the measure of the spiritual unfoldment of the individual, but all is controlled by the evolution of the soul. That is the decisive factor. The body is but the servant of the spirit, it is not the master."

The guide was asked this question: "Cannot we, through healing, influence the physical mind through the spirit-self in healing?" The reply was: "The physical mind is but the servant of the spirit. If you get the spirit mind to work, all the rest will follow. But if the spirit has not attained the stage of evolution where it can respond then you cannot make it work. What you achieve is very good, to have the body put right. But it is much more important that the soul shall come into its own, and by bringing it into touch with itself you place it upon the road of understanding. The body itself is a complicated piece of machinery, and the spirit, too, is full of many facets. All of these are subject to laws that work within laws. Whilst harmony reigns throughout, within the framework of these laws there is plenty of interplay and the one reacts upon the other."

Here, then, is the postulate upon which all healing rests: that it must subscribe to the laws that govern life in its widest sense. No healing can take place unless it is subject to influence and forces with the law.

Corrective influences are thought directives. These too may well come within the category of "energy" in a prescribed form. Thought is definite; it is not words. Words are only the means by which the consciousness translates a thought into a recognisable experience by the physical mind. For example, suppose the thought of a pencil was conveyed to a dozen different people each knowing only their own language. The thought would be received by all by the same characterised form of energy the pencil represents, but each would interpret it by the word represented in their language. This helps us to understand how people of all races can be rightly influenced from Spirit in absent healing, irrespective of language.

Every healing is an individually planned act, carried out by an individual spirit guide for the particular needs of the sufferer, within the law. This is the simple logical basis on which every healing depends. The methods are many and the implications that arise present a most fascinating series of problems for the thinker. This basis is as factual as the act of healing. We are forced to accept these facts from proven experience. We are able to add to this foundation by conclusions that arise from the study of healing experiences. We see the changes that take place consistent with, and dated by, the intervention of spiritual healing. This enables us to build from the base a reasoned hypothesis as to the methods employed by the guides in overcoming the causes and symptoms of disease.

If this book has done but a little to achieve this, then it will have contributed its part to a better appreciation of the motives that activate spiritual healing. These are the strengthening of those good forces which can be mobilised to play a still more impressive part in the eternal conflict of good against evil, the furtherance of the divine plan that began with God's creation.

INDEX